"This brilliant guide on revision is guaranteed to improve your novel and your storytelling power overnight. I don't say 'overnight' lightly. Yourke's advice is delivered in short, meaningful bites that have you nodding 'Yes, I can do that and I will do that to improve my novel.' The 'can-do' tone makes it impossible to deny trying Yourke's simple-yet-powerful creative tricks for everything from improving your characters and concept, to sentence structures and voice. The guide presents a bounty of before-and-after examples on almost every page. Her 'Character Presence' method—laid out step-by-step with many examples, too—was an eye-opener. The CP method gives mastery to novelists who want to dive deep into the many facets of point of view, characterization, and their own writing style. Her CP method helps ferret out paragraph-level mistakes common in early drafts and rejected manuscripts. A highly recommended resource guide for serious novelists and MFA students."

> — **CHRISTINE DESMET**, author, Master Class teacher/faculty associate in writing and director of the "Write-by-the-Lake Writer's Workshop & Retreat" at University of Wisconsin-Madison

"I wish that *Beyond the First Draft* had been available when I wrote my first novel. I wouldn't have spent near as much time bumbling and stumbling through several revisions—and learning the hard way how important revision and re-writing are to creating a readable novel. What the novelist needs to know about how to move beyond the first draft is on these pages. From 'plotting the plot,' to 'voice' and 'character.'"

> — **JERRY APPS**, author of seven novels, the most recent *Cold as Thunder*, University of Wisconsin Press, 2018.

"As a writing teacher with nineteen years' experience, I know how difficult it can be to convince students of the importance of revision. From the 'Ten Fictions about Fiction' to the 'Ten Writing Commandments,' Laurel Yourke's user-friendly book makes the case that rewriting is writing at its most engaging. With specific examples from top-selling literary fiction, *Beyond the First Draft* illustrates each concept it advocates—such as 'harnessing verbs' and implementing strategic telling—and provides accessible and intuitive checklists throughout. The growth among my student writers in understanding the personal narrative has encouraged me to acquire this book for my school and to recommend this title to other AP teachers and University of Minnesota faculty I know."

> — **MARA COREY**, AP English and University of Minnesota faculty

Beyond
the
First Draft

LAUREL YOURKE

Beyond the First Draft

DEEP NOVEL REVISION

Wyatt-MacKenzie Publishing
DEADWOOD, OREGON

Beyond The First Draft
Deep Novel Revision

Laurel Yourke, Ph.D.

ISBN: 978-1-942545-98-9
Library of Congress Control Number: 2017956605

Wyatt-MacKenzie Publishing
DEADWOOD, OREGON

Wyatt-MacKenzie Publishing, Inc.
Deadwood, Oregon
info@wyattmackenzie.com

Dedication

To every writer seeking the "vision" in revision

Table of Contents

Preface

Let's say you've completed a draft of your novel. Despite enthusiasm, you perhaps warily realize that you'll have to revise. Maybe you wonder "what now?" If so, you resemble most of the writers I've met during forty years of coaching.

I always offer them my own writing "bibles." Robert McKee is brilliant on scenario. John Truby knows all about theme, while Noah Lukeman and Sol Stein are experts on tension. Then there's Jack Bickham on scene, Lisa Cron on the psychology of narrative, David Jauss on the author/narrator/character distinction, Donald Maass on surprise, and Jessica Page Morrell on editing.

These books are instructional and inspiring. But not a single one is exclusively geared toward polishing and revising. The writers I coach kept asking me to write the book they needed on their shelf. So I did.

Beyond the First Draft tackles revision, a process that overwhelms many serious writers. Where do you start? How do you maintain the creative fire of the unrestricted first draft? Daunted, writers often spend less time revising structure than on improving the quality of the adjectives. Does any of that sound familiar? Help is at hand.

My experience at conferences, with critique groups, and in classrooms and living rooms has produced a book's worth of solutions to revision issues. My approach dispels the many writing myths out there. Is it really true that you should "never, ever tell"? "Just be yourself" is actually more suitable for a diary. This book combines insight from the numerous writing texts I've explored with wisdom from the highly skilled writers I've had the privilege of coaching.

My relationship with "my" writers is symbiotic. I coach them—but no more than they coach me. Their needs and skills resulted in the new theory that this book introduces. Readers need the narrator and character, the intimate and panoramic, and the characters' actions plus their emotions. Yet the most talented novelists weren't consistently offering this. How could I help?

Sentence by sentence, the Character Presence (CP) system asks the writer to consider the reader's experience. The result of this system? Greater objectivity. A balanced fictional world. More dynamic tension, suspense, empathy, and momentum.

But CP theory is only part of revision, which includes everything from scenario to scene to sentence. Through analysis, examples, checklists, and exercises, you'll explore the benefits of integrating plotting with marketing, along with an overview of characterization, pace, point of view, causality, and dialogue. You'll end with voice: knowledge of craft must never overpower the wildness that liberates it.

Revision is hard work. Humor and encouragement make hard work easier, don't they? The ideas in this book both motivate and reflect a thriving fiction-writing community. With this book, you can join us. I hope you will.

Revisiting Revision
from Scenario to Scene to Sentence

A first draft offers uncensored freedom, possibly making the revision that follows seem tedious, painful, or even discouraging. Where'd the exhilaration go? If only you could start another book instead. On the other hand, perhaps revising excites you. But what if all you see is what you hope you wrote?

Novels need suspense, dimension, electricity, and rhythm. There's more. Characters must compel and scenes sizzle.

●◆ **Scene**: a dramatic interaction that engages reader emotions, usually involves more than one character, and changes at least one character psychologically, morally, or both.

How to accomplish all that? Where to start?

Not to worry. Revise deeply rather than superficially, and you'll add tension, humor, and surprise to every page. The process begins with rigorous objectivity.

> **TIP**
> To revise your novel effectively, you must see it clearly.

Albert Einstein observed that redefining a problem helps solve it. This applies equally well to fiction and revising it. The issue is perception, and the definitions and concepts from this book will help you read your words the way a stranger would.

"Vision" is the most important component of revision. You'll examine your novel from unexpected angles to discover strategic opportunities and innovative solutions. The work becomes efficient, gratifying, possibly exhilarating.

Instead of fiddling with individual word choices, you'll tackle structural issues. As you proceed, why not combine marketing with revising? Then you merge the business of writing with the polishing of it.

Deep revision requires discarding some familiar myths about plot, setting, *telling*, sentence fragments, and narrator versus characters. So you can diagnose more insightfully. You'll also discover an objective system for evaluating what individual sentences contribute. Or don't.

But of course diagnosis is only the start. Each chapter follows analysis with problem-solving tools and techniques. With that for support, nothing can stop you from transforming your novel into everything you hoped it would be. Whether you've completed one, two, or twenty-two drafts, this book helps you polish every aspect of your novel—from scenario to scene to sentence. Here goes.

TIP

Wonder whether something you wrote is good enough? You already know the answer.

The Marketplace

Revision as Inspiration

Why write a novel? Why read a book on revising a novel? Because you love your characters. Because you love the idea that readers will love your characters. Revision makes that happen. So it can—and should—be an act of love.

Yet revision often terrifies, perhaps for reasons like these.

- Aren't novelists born, not made?
- Won't I drain all the energy from my pages?
- How do I fix what needs fixing?
- What if I make my book worse instead of better?
- How do I tackle everything at once?

The myths surrounding revision can magnify it into a powerful adversary. But there's no need for anxiety. Make a plan. Follow it. It's that simple.

TIP

Revision helps you polish in order to publish.

This book neutralizes the fictions about fiction by articulating each myth, then counteracting it with practical techniques and exercises. Here's an overview:

Ten Fictions about Fiction, and How to Offset Them

#1

False: Outlines stifle creativity.
True: Planning reduces frustration.
(See Chapter 1.)

#2

False: In first person point of view, the author, narrator, and character are identical.
True: In every point of view, these roles differ at least slightly. (See Chapters 2 and 6.)

#3

False: Never, ever *tell*.
True: Essentials delivered in voice aren't *telling*.
(See chapters 2, 3 and 10.)

#4

False: The main plot and subplots are loosely related.
True: A novel is a unified whole.
(See chapters 3 and 4.)

#5

False: Readers love easing in, so it's impossible to start a *scene* too early.
True: Begin dramatically—every time.
(See chapters 4 and 5.)

#6

False: Every moment of a novel should be in scene.
True: For faster pace, compress what can't captivate.
(See chapter 5.)

#7

False: Transitions bore readers.
True: Provide a tour guide for your fictional world.
(See chapter 5.)

#8

False: When characters ponder emotions and decisions, you add tension.
True: Actions speak louder than words.
(See chapters 3 and 7.)

#9

False: Long or unclear sentences won't matter so long as the plot works.
True: Sentence structure affects tension and suspense.
(See chapter 9.)

#10

False: Voice is entirely a matter of luck and innate talent.
True: Voice blends talent with craft and courage.
(See chapter 10.)

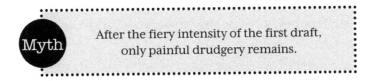

Myth After the fiery intensity of the first draft, only painful drudgery remains.

The Fable of the Swinging Kitchen Door

Revision frustrates most writers at least occasionally. Frustration can breed rationalization, which writers exploit as shrewdly as everyone else. Instead of changing how or how often you revise, why not change your perception of the process? Revision isn't a tedious cleanup after a lovely dinner; it's the exciting culmination.

To illustrate, imagine a homey farm kitchen. The door's ajar between the lively place where folks cook and eat and the pantry protecting rows of jars from sunlight. The warm, inhabited area represents your first draft, a space perfumed with the fragrance of simmering tomato sauce. Mom chuckles as she brandishes a stirring spoon in the face of a child teasing her. It's a relaxed, spontaneous, and non-judgmental world where dreams are born and fed.

Revision's on the other side of the swinging kitchen door. People come here to find what they need and get things done. Perhaps this space feels less creative than deciding what to make or how to season it. After the happy chaos of cooking, restoring order to the cabinets or hunting down the peaches might seem dull.

But it's a swinging door! The rough draft produced in the sunlight is just one push away from the pantry. Did you toss everything together the first time? You'll have to discard some unsalvageable concoctions. You might have to visit the cupboards for new supplies. That needn't banish revision out into the cold. A swinging door means that the good times don't end when the first draft does.

> **TIP**
> Revision is an opportunity to complete the novel you love.

Avoiding Surface Skim

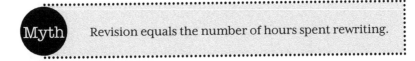

Myth Revision equals the number of hours spent rewriting.

Not necessarily. Real revision is real work. After the impetuous, exhilarating trial and error of a first draft, you must interweave each plot event until removing even one thread unravels the entire tapestry. Some novelists postpone that challenge by becoming expert researchers, tinkerers, or housekeepers. After even the cat box sparkles, you might continue reworking the opening. Or squander precious revision time substituting "beneath" for "under," then restoring "under." Fine, but that's not deep revision.

Deep Revision: Diagnosing and strengthening characterization and plot.

> In contrast, surface revision, or the "thesaurus syndrome," lets you procrastinate.

Thesaurus Syndrome: Altering individual words instead of revising deeply.

> The thesaurus syndrome is like attacking termites with fresh paint and a fancy towel rack. Decorate only after implementing essential repairs. Word choice and sentence structure don't begin the revision process—they finish it.

TIP

Create a solid structure before addressing anything else.

Revising Your Attitude toward Revising

Why did your novel steal your heart? How much do you care about it?

True/False Questionnaire

1. As a perfectionist, I struggle with most tasks longer than necessary.

> Many people finish their novels either too soon or late. If you tend to overdo, give yourself a deadline. If you bore easily, remember that agents and editors bore even more easily.

2. I love challenges.

> Those who love challenges are lucky. Does contemplating them make you want to nap? Then focus on polishing your story. One step at a time.

3. If I'm washing the windows, I don't mind a couple of streaks.

> Clean your windows however you want, but offer readers a clear view.

4. Transitions between *scenes* are tedious, so I don't bother with them.

> Explaining why you cut corners sends agents/publishers running—in the wrong direction.

Using Your Responses

Any attitudes you want to revise? Analyze your motivation, as well. Do you seek an agent or publisher? Readers? A book of high quality? An impressive advance? All of the above?

Why not jot down your answers, because the ego that drives writing often assails writers with doubt. "Am I working hard enough?" "Is my story good enough?" "Am I good enough?"

Most writers experience at least some of that at least some of the time. If you ever feel fragile, concentrate on your characters instead of yourself.

Ten Writing Commandments

These facilitate deep revision and a healthy attitude toward the process.

1. Compare yourself only to yourself.

2. Read your work as a reader would.

3. Remember that negativity obstructs creativity.

4. Critique your work as respectfully as you would someone else's.

5. Memorize compliments from those you respect.

6. Value your story as much as its publication.

7. Respect your instincts about what doesn't work, no matter how much time you spent on it. Maybe it took all that time because it was always wrong.

8. Start every chapter with real trouble.

9. End every chapter except the last with even worse trouble.

10. Design a revision plan, but implement it flexibly.

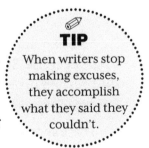

TIP
When writers stop making excuses, they accomplish what they said they couldn't.

Be your own writing partner. That means not only critiquing, but nurturing. Partnering also includes scheduling, perhaps at least fifteen minutes each day. Anyone can do fifteen minutes! Feeling stuck? Pay no attention. Just get to work. You might be surprised at how your mood changes once you're writing instead of thinking about writing.

Here's the beauty of designing a revision plan. Even in fifteen minutes, many writers can actually accomplish something. Twenty, anyhow.

Thinking about the Shrinking Fiction Market

As business people and book lovers, agents and publishers weigh quality against risk. So don't bother second-guessing. Beautiful writing won't automatically sell your book. But it can't hurt.

Dejection, however, can. So many writers give up too easily, unable to take the gigantic step from completing a book to selling it. How do you feel about that?

Myth

Agents and editors know exactly what they want and disregard everything else.

True/False Marketing Attitude Test

1. I want my novel to be good. What's considered success doesn't matter.

> If really does matter, why not admit that. In any case, deep revision tackles both craft and marketing necessities.

2. I expect financial reward for my effort and time.

> Can't wait to quit your day job? Consider writing nonfiction. It sells faster.

3. I want to spend my time writing. That's the whole point, isn't it?

> Writers become writers because they love words and stories, not because they're dying to market anything, much less themselves. But readers don't read books they never heard of. Make sure they hear about yours.

4. Publication determines the value of my time, my novel and my—self.

> Business is about business, not self-worth. And don't quit too soon. John Grisham, Stephen King, and J.K. Rowling received numerous rejections, as did Nobel winner William Faulkner and blockbuster novelist Margaret Mitchell. Fortunately, self-publication no longer requires apology. Want your book out there? Do what that takes.

An Exercise Routine

You can apply every concept in this book without completing a single exercise. Still, exercises curb rationalization while eliminating the pressure of perfection. Isn't that a strategic approach to repairing any weaknesses?

TIP

There's always a home for great new novels and novelists.

The exercises in this book encourage the brainstorming that swings the kitchen door between inspiration and insight. If you try at least the exercises that tempt you, your discoveries might prove surprising.

Making a Plan

You probably couldn't accomplish this even if you wanted to, and why would you? However unintentionally, writing commandments often confuse or mislead. Isn't there an exception to any "rule" you ever heard? You'll revise most happily and successfully if you see this book as a set of guidelines—not a stultifying prison of "should" or "should not."

Myth

List every writing rule you ever heard and methodically address them all.

The most successful revision journeys combine planning with elasticity and optimism. Mix or match from the strategies below.

#1

Listen to your story.

Articulate what you love, love, love about your project. Then be honest about why others might love it less. Some writers achieve greater objectivity by printing hard copies and revising on paper. Others type a cue like "bbb" as a reminder to return and address later. But fix what needs fixing instead of hoping it's better than it seems.

#2

Identify priorities.

Tackle them one by one, proceeding by *scene*, chapter, or several passes through the novel as a whole. Try questions like these:

- Which event propels the entire journey?
- Does the mid-section include sufficient action, tension, and emotion?
- Do inescapable pressures motivate the main characters to change?
- What's the purpose of each *scene*?
- Is the resolution of the ending earned?
- Does the plot deliver the theme?
- Do all the details add?
- Are you satisfied with style, voice, wording, and sentence structure?

#3

Create a storyboard.

Screenwriters often map the title and purpose of each *scene*, either with index cards or a huge chart online or on the wall. This lets you proceed in any order, evaluating the contribution of each *scene*. The technique works equally well for fiction.

#4

Compose an outline.

Maybe IIIs and ds annoy you. Don't let that stop you. A brief, casual form of outline clarifies the relationships between key elements. But only if you omit extraneous details, Drivers get lost in "Look for the gold 'On Tap' sign in this little copse of trees after the sixth traffic light, before the red barn." Distractions get writers lost, too.

#5

Intensify the obstacles your characters face.

Hamlet's plight drives a lot of novels:

> The time is out of joint. O cursed spite,
>
> That ever I was born to set it right!

To repair a broken world, the protagonist must renounce personal comfort and safety. The more you torture the protagonist you love, the more tension and thus emotion you add to every page. Keep this in mind as you revise.

And so...

Like everyone else, writers succumb to procrastination and rationalization. Do you love your story enough to replace the *thesaurus syndrome* with deep revision?

That requires objectivity. Do the plot and characters entice while the narrator guides? Do personal intrusions disappear from its pages? Do you ever upstage your novel?

TIP
A little planning can curtail a lot of frustration.

Some writers find this suggestion counter-intuitive. It's my novel, of course it's me. Yes, but only through your characters and narrator. The next chapter analyzes the triangle of author, character, and narrator and how that facilitates deep revision.

Deep Revision Tip

#1

The more you enjoy revising, the better you'll revise.

2

The Players

Author, Characters, and Narrator

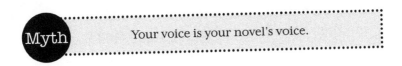

Myth Your voice is your novel's voice.

Everyone has more than one voice. Grief or anger changes it, as does public speaking versus conversing, brainstorming, composing, or revising. If novelist Jenny Smith creates a Lucy who exactly replicates Jenny, Jenny's in worse trouble than Lucy ever could be.

Fiction shouldn't exactly reproduce a single thing. Story's task and goal is a simulation of reality, or verisimilitude. Imitation, rather than replication, devises the characters and narrator who make fiction more thrilling, credible, and moral than reality.

Narrator: Persona guiding readers along the fictional journey.

Story combines characters and narrator to convey the world that readers traverse. For millennia now, narrators have cast spells, creating territory more believable, reasonable, and ethical than reality.

Unlike characters, narrators earn their keep performing the tough tasks of positioning, bridging, disclosing, and unifying. That's heavy lifting for faint praise. The narrator dispenses what the author mustn't articulate and the characters don't know. This includes causality.

Causality: a plot where each event instigates the next, forcing characters to face the consequences that foster maturation and earn the ending.

In fiction, punishment or reward stems not from coincidence but from decisions and actions. A series of ill-advised choices causes the climax and reinforces the theme.

Who underscores this causality? The narrator, whose contribution rivals the heroics of any character.

Unlike people or characters, the narrator's sole purpose is storytelling. This other-directed stance distinguishes the narrator from either the author or the author's characters. *Vive la difference*, because the storyteller—not the author—gives characters to readers.

Yet narrators need to remain backstage. Unable to kiss, shriek, or kick, they must compensate with voice appeal alone. Create that by handling your narrator like a character. You've pictured the characters slashing invaders or lacing corsets. Imagine your narrator slashing extraneous details and lacing vividness into description or backstory.

> **TIP**
> Use the voices of your characters and narrator to release your own.

Readers associate fiction with its characters. But its narrators are the unsung heroes, and their voices must captivate accordingly.

Author, Narrator, and Character Contrasted

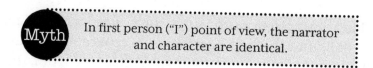

Myth In first person ("I") point of view, the narrator and character are identical.

Characters act and decide. Narrators clarify. Just as the storytelling persona differentiates the narrator from the author, the narrator's role sets the narrator apart from any character in any point of view. Even when the narrator and character share the same name, the storyteller already knows the character's fate. The narrator, who doesn't live the story, lets readers do so vicariously. The sole (and rare) exception is a present-tense novel conveying events as they occur rather than afterwards, such as Stephen L. Carter's *The Emperor of Ocean Park*.

Aside from novels like Carter's, while characters flee the trouble banging on the door, the untroubled narrator calmly illuminates that trouble. Characters blunder; narrators analyze blundering. Authors blunder, too, either by intruding, or creating characters and narrator either too close together or far apart.

Of course the author, narrator, and character overlap, but never completely. Here's that breakdown:

● **Identity.**

Author: Person creating the story.

Character: Fictitious person living the story.

Narrator: Fictitious persona delivering the story.

● **Knowledge of Outcome.**

Author: Nails the plot's resolution eventually.

Character: Struggles until the plot's resolution.

Narrator: Knows the plot's resolution in advance.

● **Goal.**

Author: Achieve success in the real world.

Character: Achieve success in the fictional world.

Narrator: Frame the fictional world for readers in the real world.

● **Relationship to time.**

Author: Exists in literal time.

Character: Exists in *scenes* or flashbacks.

Narrator: Exists outside time with the power to speed or slow it.

● **Sense of self.**

Author: Vacillates between confidence and insecurity in the real world.

Character: Vacillates between confidence and insecurity in the fictional world.

Narrator: Focuses on audience and is neither confident nor insecure.

● **Worldview.**

Author: Invested in theme.

Character: Uninterested in theme.

Narrator: Illustrates theme through plot.

These parallels and discrepancies reflect a wise narrator who doesn't act and an unwise character who must: a terrific recipe for fiction.

TIP
The author/ narrator/character triangle operates in every point of view.

Balancing Author Power

Myth The author drives the story.

As author you're the puppeteer, master of ceremonies, Big Kahuna. Yet, if, presumably, absolute power corrupts absolutely, power can seduce you into competing with your own novel. Even with the most famous authors, the soul of fiction is never the author, but, rather, characters enacting a plot and a narrator grounding it. Where's the author? Behind the scenes.

Still, ego affects everyone. Including authors. Novelists sometimes abuse power by upstaging the characters or narrator. Research, memories, antipathies, passions, or fantasies about Pulitzers and film rights can overwhelm story. Of course ego inspires the first draft and tackles the challenges of revision, publication, and marketing. But a healthy ego lets readers enjoy the characters and narrator—not the author.

TIP
Disappear inside your story.

Balancing Character Power

Myth Great characters are all a novel needs.

Readers adore characters chasing wealth, white whales, romance, or righteousness. And those characters sometimes rebel because they know themselves better than the author does. If that happens, congratulate yourself on the living beings you developed, and consider the plot twists your creations inspire.

Characters drive novels because they offer certain assets:

- **Visibility**
- **Accessibility**
- **Emotion**
- **Vulnerability**
- **Heroism**
- **Universality**

But characters can't or won't admit everything. Narrators complete the picture, making Don Quixote, Jane Eyre, or Harry Potter more understandable and thus memorable than they'd otherwise be.

TIP

Novels need characters acting and emoting plus a narrator guiding.

Unless a narrator provides context, motivation, and theme, flat characters inhabit a one-dimensional world. By supplying background, narrators compensate for the possibility of character subjectivity, self-pity, arrogance, or cluelessness.

Balancing Narrator Power

Myth A good narrator is an invisible one.

Just as the author mustn't overpower the narrator, the narrator mustn't overpower the characters. Though narrators aren't the story itself, they do frame it. Where would story be without logistics, complex emotions, and crucial background? Of course frames should never conflict or distract. The narrator must support and enhance the picture—not the other way around.

Readers want—and need—that frame. One step removed from the plot, the narrator supplements character behavior or emotion by supplying what readers can't infer. When the narrator fulfills the role of illuminating, there's no *telling* involved.

●◆ *Telling*: Dispensing judgments or conclusions that readers would prefer to infer.

Whenever narrator analysis intrudes, however, readers perceive it as *telling*. Obviously, the narrator mustn't repeat, judge, or comment if the characters can perform the *showing* themselves.

●◆ *Showing*: Events and details that permit vicarious experience and thus reader inference.

Narrators themselves can't *show*, since they never face the worst case scenario of "a perfect storm," either at sea or between the sheets. Because of this, narrators sometimes overstate, teach, and preach. They might condescend or prattle on.

This makes many novelists uneasy about narrator interference. So writers sometimes attempt to conceal the narrator entirely. This response is partially legitimate. But instead of dreading the nondescript narrator because of potential problems, why not create one who delights? To do that, assume a persona, a word derived from "mask."

Mask. Visualize 18th century Venice, where elaborate disguises permitted intrigue and illicit liaisons. Even today, masks conjure camouflage, flirtation, and suspense—the very reasons people love novels. Successful authors entice readers from behind the mask of a captivating narrator.

A strong narrator enjoys the same right to visibility as a novel's characters. For example, in a historical work like Ken Follett's *The Pillars of the Earth*, readers want even more than the vicarious experience of encountering young boys waiting around for a hanging while making cruel remarks about it. The narrator's chilling indictment of their inhuman callousness actually shocks even more than the scene itself.

Characters and narrator respectively perform certain roles. Both are necessary to complete the reader's experience.

TIP

Do it with a mask.

Yet to be successful, narrators must dispense context charismatically. Like a poem neither excessively clear nor ambiguous, the narrator reveals rather than obscuring, oversimplifying, or judging. This means eliminating overused, vague, or abstract description such as an "angry" argument, "large" town, or "fateful" journey.

Narrator Tasks

Heroes transform by accepting missions. Narrators transform by making the commonplace exotic and the alien accessible. Ever since Homer evoked the muse at the opening of the *Iliad*, narrators have grounded, interpreted, and disclosed or withheld secrets.

When your narrator informs without seeming to, you let readers imagine the unimaginable. The horror of slavery defies comprehension. In *The Known World*, Edward P. Jones lets us taste that horror by describing how eating dirt defines the parameters of self and world for the slave Moses. Readers don't just watch the man literally eat dirt. Because of the narrator, they grasp what this action means to him, how it completes his sense of self.

Narrators can offer the nuance and insight that few characters possess. Unless the author intrudes with an info-dump, context can prove a welcome addition. Tim O'Brien, in *The Things They Carried*, conveys the stench of war not with what the characters say or do but with what they require to survive physically—and emotionally.

A narrator's tone, in this case, journalistic, often adds a layer of suffering not otherwise available. Generally, when the situation is tragic, you'll elicit the greatest empathy by keeping the language neutral and avoiding any hint of melodrama.

Regardless of tone, a visible narrator is riskier than a nondescript one. To play it safe, never tell, repeat, pose too many questions, or mock those willing to pay $29.99 for the hardcover.

Yet excessive caution can thwart excellence. The N.Y. Times ranked Jonathan Franzen's rule-smashing *Freedom* among the top five novels of its publication year—substantially due to a strong narrator who is visible for part of every page.

What's this narrator like? Franzen's storyteller introduces punctilious characters posing obnoxious questions. Then why read this? Because the greatest drama usually occurs in the territory where every rule gets broken—but no one minds. Few write like Franzen, or want to, or should. Yet every author ought to know the narrator well enough to create one who can be brazenly present. At least occasionally.

TIP

Readers receive the best experience when the narrator and characters fulfill their respective roles.

And so...

People write novels to interpret a behavior, location, idea, or belief. Yet novelists must communicate indirectly through the narrator and characters; any trace of the author catapults readers from the fiction you worked to create.

Authors usually realize that like most people, they're occasionally opinionated or boring and must disappear inside story. That's slightly sad, but beautiful, too, because narrators and characters—not authors—bestow the gift of plot.

The contrast between a wise narrator and misguided characters escalates tension and supports theme. As the characters enact the plot, readers experience an emotional rollercoaster right along with those enduring it. At the end, readers discover what the narrator hinted from the start.

But, without the narrator's guidance, readers might miss many subtleties. The narrator escorts readers through the characters' world, offering entertainment, fore-shadowing, and synthesis. Good narrators manage all that and more. That's how they deliver story, which is the next chapter's topic.

Deep Revision Tip

#2

Like most tasks, deep revision depends on the right tool at the right time.

3

Storytelling

The Human Gift and Responsibility

Story is intrinsically human. Its structure has remained stable since Aristotle foretold how characterization, plot, and metaphor would operate in the genres born centuries after his death.

➥ **Genre**: A particular category, which might refer to poetry, film, or fiction, or a subcategory of one, such as young adult, fantasy, romantic suspense, historical, mystery, etc.

The Greek philosopher Plato despised the story genre. In *The Republic,* he lauded the authenticity of history, advocating the banishment of all storytellers from the ideal city as he conceived it. His pupil Aristotle disagreed, valuing both the higher truths of story and the craft used to deliver them. Fortunately for us, his response was *The Poetics.*

Plato exaggerated the storyteller's power, however. As poet W.H. Auden observed, the world's legislators are the secret police, not the poets—or playwrights, or novelists. Still, fiction convinces in a way that facts can't. Because our response to it is hard-wired. The glory of story is its hidden purpose: to illuminate and instruct while entertaining.

"Lying" to Tell the Truth

Fiction writers don't exactly lie. But what is fiction if not embellishing and tampering with literal truth? This is precisely Plato's argument. Stories alter "what really happened" into a vehicle for conveying psychology and morality. Fiction writers reach readers through the characters enacting a plot (mostly *showing*) and the narrator guiding, which sometimes necessitates *telling*, or at least what's associated with that term.

17

The *show/tell* issue can make the phrase "tell me a story" sound negative. And of course storytelling needn't include a single sentence that readers don't want to read. But "spin a yarn" or "recount a narrative" are clumsy substitutes. So in this book the references to "storyteller" and "storytelling" refer not to *telling* versus *showing* but to characters and narrators fulfilling their respective roles within the fiction genre.

Tell Me a Story: From Theatre to Fiction to Film

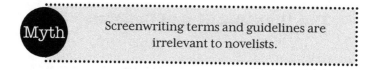

Myth Screenwriting terms and guidelines are irrelevant to novelists.

Every story, from glowering Ahab to spunky Katniss, follows character progress toward happiness or doom. No matter how literary the enterprise, plot drives story. After all, the 16th century word "novel" evolved from "romance," evoking the heroics, mystery, and passion that word still summons. Centuries later, novelists must be more like screenwriters, who focus on what characters <u>do</u>.

Membership in the storytelling tribe is both privilege and responsibility: the power to persuade combined with the obligation to charm. The scenario you design to reach those goals is what screenwriters call "concept."

Concept: The heightened dramatization of the central conflict, whether quest, love affair, success story, or moral correction.

TIP
Screenwriting reminds novelists to keep plot prominent.

Hollywood may not figure in your dreams, but *concept* marries plot to theme, whether on paper or on screen. In good stories, the plot deepens understanding of our world.

Motion to Capture Emotion

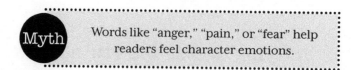

Myth Words like "anger," "pain," or "fear" help readers feel character emotions.

In screenwriting, action must convey character emotion. Novelists possess additional options. This doesn't mean that character thoughts and feelings should be the primary, much less exclusive, emphasis. *Tell* readers that a character is sad, and the response you get is irritation.

To illustrate, which of these evokes more emotion in you?

> Death is hard to picture, because it happens in solitude, feels vague and slightly uncomfortable, yet overwhelms you in a way that makes you not want to bother struggling.

versus

> I have wrestled with death. It is the most unexciting contest you can imagine. It takes place in an impalpable greyness, with nothing underfoot, with nothing around, without spectators, without clamour, without glory, without the great desire of victory, without the great fear of defeat, in a sickly atmosphere of tepid scepticism, without much belief in your own right, and still less in that of your adversary. —Joseph Conrad, *Heart of Darkness*

The first example states the obvious. In contrast, Conrad captures an entirely new way to imagine death. He makes the moment of potential finality tangible. He begins with a featureless landscape then lets readers picture the fight against an enemy who doesn't seem substantial. Conrad transforms the indescribable, making readers feel that yes, it can be described. The imagery this author constructs isn't easily dismissed.

If you continue brainstorming until you find the image you need, and then develop that image fully, you can deepen reader understanding. Imagery is the best means of portraying love, pain, death, and all those other generalities that people have trouble defining.

Tangible details, particularly if used symbolically, can impart a clarity that's not available in any other way. What about this image portraying how people move through the world:

> Experience is never limited, and it is never complete; it is an immense sensibility, a kind of huge spider-web of the finest silken threads suspended in the chamber of consciousness, and catching every air-borne particle in its tissue. —Henry James, *The Art of Fiction*

How often do we compare life to a "spider-web"? Yet, if you think about it—the fragility, the way random material falls into your purview and sticks there—makes sense. The image, too, might stick in your mind, because it's so much more effective than this observation: existence is delicate and affected by whatever passes by.

Concrete details evoke the strongest and longest-lasting reader response.

●❖ **Concrete**: An image one can see, hear, taste, touch, smell or any combination of these.

Imagery stimulates the imagination in ways that abstract generalization never can.

●❖ **Abstract**: A condition or idea, such as "fury" or "war," accessible only through intellect rather than sensation.

Authors can offer two kinds of imagery. The literal kind has a single dimension.

●❖ **Literal**: Factual portrayal of reality.

The dictionary classifies a bluebird as "an insectivorous thrush with blue plumage, white chest and pinkish throat." A novel about an ornithologist might offer this kind of information.

Today, though, even nonfiction frequently transcends mere delivery of facts. And in fiction, facts must always connect readers to the characters and their world. Otherwise, it seems like *telling* or pontificating.

One defense against stating the obvious is imagery that's not only concrete, but also symbolic.

●❖ **Symbolic**: A figurative or metaphorical comparison different from actual reality.

For instance, if a bluebird of happiness poops in the garden, that symbolic reference adds texture and irony; it no longer refers exclusively to the garden but also to the characters and events there, and perhaps even to the entire world outside.

Similarly, if you call Beth a lioness or say that her home resembles a savannah during migration, your readers receive instant insight into Beth and her tolerance level. But whether literal or symbolic, imagery bestows direct access.

Imagery and Body Language

Along with promoting reader inference, concrete details more realistically reflect the volatile, rapid-fire shift from freeze to fight, from white-hot anger to chilling grief. Stage business can offer the physical manifestation of emotion and thought.

🔊 **Stage Business**: Gesture, movement, or body language that expresses character feelings, often to ground, clarify, or pace dialogue.

If Ann raises one eyebrow, she could be smug, astonished, or amused. The fun of fiction is deciphering what Ann feels at this moment. Why deprive your readers of that pleasure?

In contrast, words like "skepticism" or "irritation" represent unrealistic emotional shorthand.

🔊 **Emotional Shorthand**: Intangible, oversimplified abbreviation of feelings like "joy" or "rage."

These versions of Mike's response illustrate why *emotional shorthand* isn't effective.

A.) The email left Mike with a dreadful anguish he'd never previously endured.

B.) Mike's expression changed as he read the email.

C.) Seeing her husband's facial muscles contract, Ruth drew him close for a hug.

TIP

Reveal character emotions through gesture and behavior.

The first version evokes no emotion, and the second is still abstract. Only in the last one do the characters act, letting readers visualize, interpret, and empathize.

Want your novel to offer cinematic moments? Provide not just wit, wisdom, and lyricism, but physicality. In *The Master*, by Colm Toibin, Tito and Henry mourn their friend's death, deciding to commemorate it by tossing her clothes through the open window into the canal outside her apartment.

Under a cloudy Venice sky, Tito and Henry recoil as dark shapes rise up from the lagoon. It's her clothes, they realize. As the garments fill with water, they billow up to the surface, as if declining to be buried, to let go. While Henry yells to leave her dresses floating there, Tito refuses. Over and over, he prods with the gondola pole, thrusting her wardrobe down until only smooth dark water remains.

This description is totally visual. That's crucial, because words like "yearning" or "adoration" can't express the layers of emotion involved in saying goodbye forever. But the dead woman's clothes floating back up? That's dynamic. This farewell is strenuous and unyielding: the men must struggle to complete their work, almost as if she refuses to depart. This short *scene* deposits readers in the gondola along with Tito and Henry. Without ever mentioning a single emotion, these few paragraphs capture the full range.

TIP

"Film" emotions with words.

↪**Exercise**: Gathering Strategies from Screenplays

Use the many screenplays available on line to contrast film and print versions of the same story. Or watch a film more than once to observe how dialogue and action do all the work. Which new discoveries can you apply to your fiction?

↪**Exercise**: Cutting the Commentary

Novel readers receive both character action and thoughts. But excessive emphasis on the latter can weaken drama and audience involvement. What if you hit the jackpot and someone filmed your book? Identify some moments in your novel that would translate into voiceover.

●◆ **Voiceover**: The narrator addressing the audience directly, often at lower volume.

Revise any passages from your novel that would benefit from action instead of voiceover.

Dilemma

> **Myth**   All a great story needs is terrific characters.

Not quite. Great stories entice with at least one character in terrible trouble. Make that trouble terrible enough that the protagonist, or central character, faces a dilemma.

●◆ **Dilemma**: A compulsory choice between two unacceptable options.

What could be worse? This impossible position compels both characters and readers. This predicament originates from forcing your character into whatever she or he absolutely can't bear to do. Often, that involves a human opponent. But whether tornado, White Whale, or nemesis, a chilling antagonist is a worthy one.

●◆ **Antagonist**: Not mere obstacle or opponent but impetus for summoning the best in the protagonist.

Like real people, protagonists don't change until the antagonist forces that. This pressure makes the character's journey more believable, meaningful, suspenseful, and touching.

Instead of giving your protagonist an easy out, or reminding readers of evil's existence, dramatize the ambiguous nature of morality. Dilemma comes from the impossibility of making a good choice. Can love survive without integrity? Does wealth bring happiness? Is betrayal ever forgivable?

Raise the stakes. Perhaps an alcoholic daughter, who blames her now-sober father for destroying her life, will discuss forgiveness only over bourbon. Or a priest must choose between the sixth Commandment and the justice denied his murdered sister.

> **TIP**
> Dilemma makes characters surprise themselves, along with authors and readers.

✔ **Checklist Exercise**: Escalating Dilemma

☐ Is your novel's main conflict simply troublesome or a heart-wrenching dilemma?

☐ Do you force the protagonist into choices where something must be lost?

☐ Is your protagonist's eventual escape from this dilemma credible?

If any of your answers dissatisfy you, revise until that's no longer the case.

The Nature of Story: 4 "Cs" from Aristotle

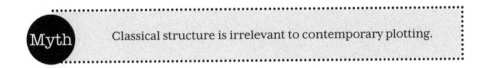

Myth — Classical structure is irrelevant to contemporary plotting.

Storytelling is storytelling, whether Oedipus gouges out his eyes or Luke Skywalker closes his to let The Force save him. Despite new genres and vast cultural changes, Aristotle's *Poetics* remains the essential guide to story versus reality, to character and plot conveying theme. One could crystallize some of this philosopher's most crucial points by analyzing characterization, credibility, causality, and coherence.

Characterization

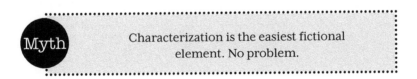

Myth — Characterization is the easiest fictional element. No problem.

The easy part is originating a protagonist from reality, imagination, or a combination of those. Multi-dimensional antagonists and protagonists are more challenging for writers but more compelling for readers. Give your protagonist the human complexity reflected in the following traits.

● Vulnerability

Nobody loves a loser. But everybody loves an underdog. Or, despite one debilitating flaw, a hero who must face the ghastly hand that fate dealt.

● Pluck

Protagonists possess the inner resources to complete the job, uncover the mystery, and win the day. Readers love watching the missteps leading to triumph the protagonist never saw coming.

● Resilience

Protagonists bounce back. They're spunky. Unless protagonists think positive, they're not worth the paper they're printed on.

● Passion

Romance is optional. Intensity isn't. Whether hunting orchids, atoms, gangsters, or love, protagonists hunger. They burn. Moderation gets tiresome quite quickly.

● Curiosity

What kills cats breeds protagonists. Denial, inertia, or caution diminish story. Sherlock Holmes endures because he never left a clue unchased.

● Universality

Fiction works because we empathize with Hector of Troy and Hester of Massachusetts Bay. Every emotion must feel like everyone's emotion, regardless of time, place, status, or genetics. Consider the unchanging nature of remorse over words unspoken or articulated far too clearly.

TIP

Compelling protagonists are both more determined and conflicted than everyone else.

⌘Exercise: Adding Character Dimension

As a warm-up, ruminate on the background of every major character in your novel: childhood, social class, hideous secrets, charming or useful attributes. Then choose four somewhat contradictory details about your protagonist, i.e. a vegetarian opera lover addicted to junk food and vacuous sit-coms. Which events and beliefs created this individual? How do conflicting tendencies complete a larger-than-life character? Don't just gather traits; integrate them.

⌘Exercise: Balancing Heroism with Vulnerability

Appealing protagonists are neither perfect nor pathetic. Open your novel with hints about the protagonist's pluck, curiosity, passion, universality, and foibles. Don't save this critical dimensionality for later on.

Credibility

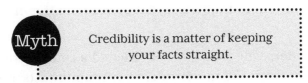

> **Myth** Credibility is a matter of keeping your facts straight.

As Mark Twain put it, "Fiction is obliged to stick to possibilities. Truth isn't." That's because fiction requires suspension of disbelief. Deliver and maintain that, and you have your readers where you want them. That power of persuasion drove Plato to suggest driving out story and its tellers.

Yet the storyteller's power is hard-won. Fiction must obey not just physics, but the implicit laws of cause and effect. Coincidence is credibility's worst enemy. Novels feel contrived when novelists insert mishap, luck, or talent as needed. Overnight rock star success can astound your protagonist, but never your readers. Nor should a contemporary deus ex machina, or divine intervention, rescue your helpless hero with a conveniently positioned ally or automatic machine gun.

> **TIP**
> Character traits and choices rather than whimsical fate must determine the fictional journey's outcome.

⌘Exercise: Planting Seeds

Once your first draft is complete, chart the skills, flaws, and interventions that the protagonist—and the author—will later need to complete the plot. Refer at least once or twice to details you'll need later. You never want readers to wonder where that twist came from.

Causality

Plot is simply what happens in your novel.

The combination of credibility and causality fosters suspension of disbelief, or willingness to accept even the most surrealistic fictional world on its own terms. Just as readers demand credibility more plausible than "but it really happened," they also want relationships tighter than "this and this and this."

In most cases, successful plots unpredictably yet inevitably progress to the good guys finishing first. When every choice triggers consequences, and every incident sparks the next, you've added causality—emphasized the relationship between impetus and outcome.

This probably won't happen automatically. The first draft is for experimenting, playing with possibilities. The decaying marriage doesn't seem like enough. You add a tornado. An uncle battling cancer. A community divided over the school referendum. Plenty of suspense, but do these isolated threads influence the main plot, or merely accompany it?

You must ask, as readers will, if you've constructed a causal plot or an interesting series of loosely linked episodes. Unless the gutted landscape affects the gutted marriage, the storyline will feel contrived. And contrived plots aren't more suspenseful or layered—just more contrived.

A causal plot helps transform your novel into a unified whole. Any event that doesn't somehow reinforce the main plot dilutes it. Besides, consequential events grip tighter than merely consecutive ones. Maybe Belinda escapes the tornado because she's with Horatio while husband Oscar drinks in the kitchen that the twister will demolish. Or Uncle Pete's death reminds Belinda that he introduced her to Oscar, so she rushes home to save him. But just barely in time.

To judge whether events impinge on each other, you might review your plot backwards—from climax back to opening. If you discover discrepancies, begin at the beginning and make each event invisibly but relentlessly propel the ending. Fortunately, causality is inherently logical and dramatic; most writers quickly internalize this approach.

TIP

Unlike the randomness of life, plot needs causality.

∞**Exercise**: Plotting Causally

Use an outline, list, or spreadsheet to trace the correlation between each event of your protagonist's journey and the decision or incident that follows. As needed, add or develop any missing causality.

Coherence

●◆ **Coherence**: Unity of the details and events in the novel.

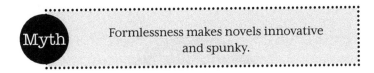

Myth — Formlessness makes novels innovative and spunky.

Disorder makes novels—chaotic. Real life frequently lacks logic and pattern. But plot needs both, which is why Aristotle restricted it to a single location within a single day. Though that structure seems too narrow for most novels, they still need coherence.

In an organic novel, every word, event, character, and detail contributes to the tapestry of the whole. To illustrate, a description of Hortense —from the ribbons on her bodice to the minor characters encountered while shopping—must support her discovery that external trappings matter less than those who create and wear them.

Yet elementary school trained us to generate every detail we could about that little red ball Ms. Raymond held up. Although the grade-school intention was to foster vocabulary and observation, as adults, novelists sometimes feel compelled to describe every bush and birdbath.

But readers follow protagonists, not their backyards. No matter how poetic, never let the details distract from what's significant. Otherwise, how can readers detect the difference?

TIP
Stay focused on the protagonist's journey.

❧**Exercise**: Choosing Relevant Details

Assess everything in your novel, from the cyclone to the canary's trill. Then, regardless of quality, cut whatever detracts from the protagonist and central plot. Yes. Truly cut.

And so...

The fun of storytelling is designing a world more interesting and convincing than the real one. That's the challenge—and the joy—of writing a novel.

Story elevates and crafts reality to the level of storytelling about reality, even if that reality is a fantastical one. The process transforms happenstance into meaningful plot by creating fiction more intriguing, believable, focused, and moral than reality.

Novels let readers escape what's tedious or discouraging about the real world. How? Characterization, credibility, causality, and coherence enhance the vulnerable yet resolute protagonist's triumph over dilemma.

You can't create a foundation like that without deep revision—honest evaluation of whether those elements work individually and in combination. Character identity causes the plot, just as plot determines character fate. The following chapter takes a long, hard look at plot—and how to market the plot you perfect.

Deep Revision Tip

#3

Deep revision, especially of plot, generates energy and inspiration.

The Big Picture
Plotting the Plot

Myth · Marketing has nothing to do with plotting.

Many novelists view composing as fun, revising as overwhelming, and marketing as nightmarish. Yet aren't they all part of one process? Integrate these stages instead of isolating them, and you'll revise more effectively and contentedly. Swing the kitchen door back and forth between inspiration and discipline.

TIP
Composing, revising, and marketing merge to complete a great novel.

Deep Structure: From Conflict to Climax

Myth · A novel's events matter more than the characters acting them out.

Millennia ago, Heraclitus observed that "Character is fate." Who you are determines what happens to you. In story, what happens is trouble. And, right up to "The End," character response, which originates in personality and identity, generates worse trouble.

Separating the characters from their journey makes little sense. It's all part of one whole, with experience affecting characters, and character nature clashing with those experiences. Like real people, characters face obstacles in the external world.

●◆ **External**: Everything that happens outside the character's mind: the setting where a novel occurs, along with character appearance and behavior.

But events in the outside world agitate the protagonist's internal world.

●◆ **Internal**: Inner or inside, as in a character's psychological conflict versus pressure from the outside.

The integrated relationship between a character's internal and external worlds is the most organic source of plot.

●◆ **Plot**: Causal incidents escalating to external climax and internal change.

Plot uses the individual to express the universal. Will Peter Cottontail curb his appetite, or ascend to rabbit heaven? In fiction, external events stimulate both rabbits and people to overcome flaws.

Deliberation about external events, though, produces neither tension nor resolution.

Scenario Structure Overview

If Lucy Landow demands a divorce because her husband hollers, readers need explanation. If Mr. Landow smacks Lucy's face with a raw chicken in front of their dinner guests, that's what Malcolm Gladwell calls the "Tipping Point." Change is inevitable: no backstory needed.

●◆ **Backstory**: Events or emotions preceding the forward journey of the plot.

Start explosively. As Aristotle said, "All human happiness and misery take the form of action." Only an inciting incident can overcome the human tendency toward inertia.

●◆ **Inciting Incident**: An explosive external event necessitating protagonist action.

TIP

To eliminate the need for backstory, the inciting incident must be self-explanatory.

As Cinderella illustrates, even fairytales begin by disrupting the norm with an inciting incident:

- **Inciting Incident**: A scullery maid hears of the upcoming ball and makes a wish.

- **Protagonist**: Not only good, good, good—but willing to take risks.

- **Antagonists**: Lazy, greedy, unappealing relatives.

- **Turning Point**: The magic evaporates, replacing fantasy with rags and a pumpkin.

- **Climax:** The charming prince finds the one foot the tiny slipper fits.

- **Theme:** Brave, small-footed nice girls finish first.

↲**Exercise**: Assessing Your Plot

Use the elements of the Cinderella scenario to overview your story. What can you intensify? Are there opportunities to instill causality that perhaps you missed?

The Enemies of Plot

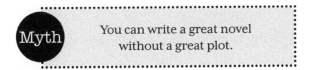

Myth · You can write a great novel without a great plot.

Possibly. But why try? Inside every novel reader is a kid excited about what happens next. Extraneous material interferes with that curiosity. Do additions like those following really add?

1. A serene, untroubled status quo.

Begin where the conflict does. Start with your novel's version of a tornado, not the ripe wheat fluttering in a soothing breeze.

2. A lush, humid, rampantly intricate and overgrown rain-forest canopy of landscape details.

Setting must support plot instead of strangling it.

3. A tangent or two plus tangential tangents generating additional tangents.

Eliminate irrelevant subplots, redundant characters, or details about auntie's first husband's neighbor's cousin's award-winning canned salmon casserole.

4. An irrelevant T-Rex, litter of kittens, garland of gardenias, or presidential pet.

Raise the stakes. Gimmicks are usually more obvious than writers hope.

5. A memory of Susan's nipple against his thigh as the fire reached the floor below him.

Locate sex scenes and innuendo logically, and remember that the cataloging of body parts can turn off more than on.

6. The kind of flabby middle no one would admire in a bathing suit.

Develop your novel's mid-section until its muscular support is enviable.

7. A miraculous rescue of the cornered hero.

Earn the ending. Protagonists—and novelists—must save themselves.

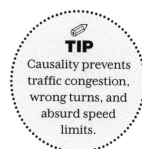

TIP
Causality prevents traffic congestion, wrong turns, and absurd speed limits.

8. An abrupt, inconclusive…

Resolve something. Queasy irresolution breeds—queasiness.

Holster versus Gunshot

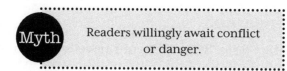

Myth   Readers willingly await conflict or danger.

Novels don't necessarily need guns. But neither does fiction need the excessive calm or context that resembles a holstered weapon. A strong opening—preferably in the first sentence—explodes with a literal or symbolic gunshot. Avoid the relaxed, happy beginning that resembles Tolstoy's famous happy families, all alike in their uninteresting tranquility.

If some bestsellers ease into conflict, it's because a name like John Grisham or subject like the Da Vinci Code discharges a symbolic pistol. Unless either your name or *concept* fires like a gun, imperil your protagonist with an inciting incident. Immediately.

∽**Exercise**: Perfecting the First Page

Maybe you've reworked your opening so often that you no longer see what's there. Grab a hat or scarf and become Ms. or Mr. New York Agent. In this role, give "the author" suggestions. Heed those you receive.

Developing a Strong Mid-Section: Causing the Climax

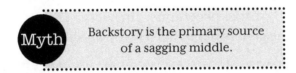

Myth · Backstory is the primary source of a sagging middle.

Only partly. Your opening sets off fireworks. Then the plot goes quiescent and murky. More than one reason underlies what's going on, or, rather, not. Which factors diminish momentum?

● **Backstory.**

Since novelists work hard to build a history, they're tempted to include it. But readers follow the future—not what brought the characters to this point. Don't you want to give readers what they want?

● **Author Attitude.**

Do you adore your novel's opening and ending and feel tepid about its middle? If so, why would your readers feel otherwise? Use the midsection to cause the climax so everyone can enjoy the entire journey.

● **Character Motivation.**

The middle holds the gold: the impetus to build arc.

●❖ **Arc**: Protagonist progress from weakness to satisfaction and maturity.

Ideally, every character you include influences the protagonist's journey toward some sort of resolution. Opposing character arcs form the spine, or novel's backbone from inciting incident to climax. A strong spine depends not just on the multi-dimensional protagonist, but on an antagonist worthy enough to elicit the protagonist's very best.

Many characters despise each other's goals while esteeming their own. Exactly like protagonists, antagonists star in the stories they tell themselves. Readers must believe every character's story, even if most antagonists lose in the end.

Sometimes interweaving arcs let both protagonist and antagonist triumph. In Jane Austen's *Pride and Prejudice*, for example, egotism keeps Darcy from seeing how Elizabeth might view his interference with her sisters' suitors. His future bride is equally misguided. But each changes enough to deserve happiness with the other.

Of course many antagonists can't change. Charles Dickens' Estella is inflexible, and she and Pip lose their "great expectations." In Victor Hugo's *Les Miserables*, the rigid Javert cannot survive the generosity of hero Jean Valjean.

Yet regardless of who wins or loses, every climax originates from antagonist pressure on the protagonist. Only a complex and credible opponent can force the protagonist to choose the path of most resistance. External force, whether human or otherwise, necessitates change and action. That's the source of a mid-section powerful enough to justify the ending. Without a compelling antagonist, that's difficult to accomplish.

∽❖**Exercise**: Creating Arcs

Plot an arc for every significant character in your novel. Now intertwine them. For example, do the characters help each other learn about freedom? Love? Justice? Happiness? If this exercise encourages foreshadowing of any choices or actions that will occur later on, set that up, though subtly.

∽❖**Exercise**: Complicating the Antagonist

Evaluate your antagonist. Is this character believable and complicated, or merely villainous? Is the antagonist powerful enough to change the protagonist?

The Pressure Cooker Plot

Change is risky. So despite discomfort or even suffering, things rattle along, building up steam. Until something makes change inevitable. Script guru Linda Seger calls this moment of psychological and dramatic coercion a pressure point.

Pressure Point: Explicit external pressure necessitating action.

Pressure points exert life-changing consequences—no turning back the clock. Because the character can't disregard what's now apparent, the choice about making a choice disappears. Yet as the *pressure points* occur, neither characters nor readers should notice their significance.

The inciting incident is usually the first *pressure point*. In most novels, four to six additional *pressure points* follow. Fewer might not create an arc, and more might feel cluttered.

Following the inciting incident, the protagonist takes the wrong action—makes the wrong choice—at each *pressure point*. Until the climax. At that last *pressure point*, the protagonist's choice again seems a mistake. Yet in most cases, it yields understanding, if not happy ever after.

Here's an illustration of *pressure points* in Herman Melville's *Moby Dick*:

- The sea lures Ishmael to enlist on the Pequod whaler. An ill-fated voyage?

- Ahab offers a gold doubloon for spotting the White Whale. A deranged captain?

- Prophet Gabriel warns about Moby Dick. A dark omen?

- Captain Boomer cautions against vengeance. A doomed ship?

- Ahab orders the harpoon baptized with human blood. Blasphemy?

- First mate Starbuck spares Ahab despite his crazed response to a typhoon striking the ship. Last chance?

These events and choices result in "the great shroud of the sea" swallowing the Pequod. Only one survivor remains to recount this fatal voyage.

Pressure points credibly and logically produce the climax. You can use them either to plan a novel or strengthen one already written.

TIP

Your novel's middle motivates and foreshadows its resolution.

Exercise: Plotting with *Pressure Points*

Identify the four to six *pressure points* of your novel. Anything you could add, substitute, motivate, or sharpen? Go for it.

Closure versus Quitting

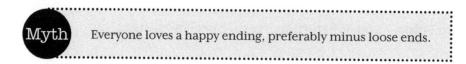

Myth Everyone loves a happy ending, preferably minus loose ends.

Actually, every 19th-century reader loved a happy ending, preferably without a single loose end. Tastes change. It's a little late for bluebirds tweeting cyber-happiness or righteous reminders about being responsible for our own. Today's readers know that rose gardens have thorns and dislike both the obvious and the obscure.

If the inciting incident and subsequent *pressure points* produce the resolution, then the protagonist's good fortune makes good sense. Construct your plot causally, and you're less likely to judge or overstate. You'll more easily resist the temptation to explain, dawdle, rush, or make miracles.

Instead, let imagery convey joy or justice. The ending of Amy Tan's *The Joy Luck Club*, for instance, replaces platitudes about forgiveness with a verbal photograph of sisters reunited—the fulfillment of a mother's wish.

TIP
Tangible imagery makes endings memorable.

Exercise: Scrutinizing Endings

Analyze the conclusions of five novels you love. Are there techniques you might adapt?

✔ **Checklist Exercise**: Reviewing Plot

☐ Does an inciting incident launch your novel?

☐ Does the inciting incident induce a chain of *pressure points*?

☐ Is the central conflict a genuine dilemma?

☐ Is any backstory brief, pertinent, and well-placed?

☐ Does the setting enhance conflict?

☐ Do you start foreshadowing your protagonist's ultimate success early on?

☐ Does the mid-section inevitably cause the climax?

☐ Do extraordinary measures ever rescue your protagonist?

☐ Is the climax surprising yet credible?

☐ Is the ending neither rushed nor sluggish?

☐ If your novel is part of a series, does its last page both conclude and entice?

Organic versus Synthetic Theme

Myth Readers dislike themes, because they're merely dated clichés about morality.

Fiction entertains with adventure, mystery, romance, lyricism, and insight. Add theme, and these pleasures engage more deeply.

●✦ **Theme**: The meaning of the characters' journeys.

An implicit theme gives a bigger bang for the price of a paperback, because genuine themes inhabit the gap between actuality and ideal. Themes appraise not only the characters' world, but our own. Hint why characters change, or remain the same. This improves both plot and publication opportunities.

Regardless of genre, readers prefer outcomes that originate not from luck, but character choices.

In every type of novel, effective themes surpass abstract oversimplifications like "Gentility comes from behavior, not social class," or "The American Dream is all smoke and mirrors." Instead, convey theme through the plot's resolution. In Dickens' *Great Expectations*, experience teaches Pip what matters. Fitzgerald's Gatsby destroys himself for golden Daisy, who is insubstantial as a sunset over Long Island Sound.

Meaningful themes don't oversimplify, belabor, stereotype, or contrive. They offer:

● **Tangibility.**

Event and imagery convince the way abstraction never can.

● **Universality.**

Genuine truths and emotions never change.

● **Implication.**

Readers love the sensation of "So that's where it was going."

● **Inspiration.**

People cling to the hope that Emily Dickinson called "the thing with feathers." Its source? Impassioned repair of damaged morality.

● **Epiphany**

The best insights reveal what we never knew we knew.

↪**Exercise**: Harnessing Imagery

Find an image to "photograph" your novel's ending. Can concrete imagery convey your theme(s)?

↪**Exercise**: Reflecting Complexity

To mirror the ambiguity of reality, replace any blatant generalities in your novel, like "always be honest," with the absolute danger of absolute honesty, as Jane Austen's Emma must discover in order to deserve Mr. Knightley.

To Market, To Market: Logline, Synopsis, and Query

Myth Why bother with marketing until you're looking for an agent or publisher.

Agents and editors expect, or at least prefer, fully polished novels. Submitting before you're ready isn't wise. Still, it's never too soon to anticipate submitting later. Your revision of plot and theme prepares you for marketing, while planning marketing improves plot and theme. This makes both tasks more efficient and meaningful.

To accomplish that, start with the logline.

●◆ **Logline:** A short, snappy summary of a novel's protagonist, dilemma, setting, and genre.

The brevity of a logline, or log, lets you play with plot while pumping gas, flossing your teeth, or daydreaming during commercials. Commercials make products shine. A successful log hints that your book offers success with minimal risk.

But the best commercials tantalize rather than mislead. They spin. That's what loglines do. Don't call your novel a "sexy thriller" if it follows two aging librarians tracing the history of the Gutenberg Bible. Instead, without changing the story you want to tell, hint that we can't live without this one.

X-Ray of a Logline

Want to attract the businesspeople who represent and publish novels? Highlight your *concept* while following convention. Use present tense and identify protagonist role. "Santiago," for example, is just a name. But an impoverished fisherman battling to reclaim his luck? That *concept* underlies Ernest Hemingway's *The Old Man and the Sea*.

In this log for Anita Shreve's *Sea Glass* (2000), *concept* raises the stakes:

> It's 1929. In an impoverished mill town by the sea, a naïve female bank teller balances marital fidelity against the passions that a deadly mill strike arouses.

Logs condense what matters. Shreve's historical novel combines social upheaval with psychological. The ocean provides a visual, while sex and danger heighten the *concept*.

☞**Exercise**: Brainstorming Your Logline

Warm up by picturing your novel at its best.

TIP
To revise plot and develop synopsis, start your logline early.

◆ Articulate your reasons for writing this novel.

◆ Pinpoint the universal elements of your protagonist's dilemma.

◆ Find vivid imagery to capture your scenario.

◆ Emphasize what readers will love about your novel.

◆ Compare your novel with successful publications.

✔ **Checklist Exercise**: Polishing Your Log

Fast as you can, jot down some logline possibilities. Ignore these attempts for at least two weeks. Then gut, smooth, and make one version do handstands until you'd rather perform one yourself. Again, wait some time without sneaking a peak. Now revise using the requirements below. Proceed as if finding an agent/publisher depends on this. Which it does.

☐ Have you conveyed your own excitement about your book?

☐ Does the *concept* sound memorable and commercially viable?

☐ Do you emphasize what's at stake and why this matters?

☐ Can you hint where to shelve your novel in a bookstore?

☐ Is the logline a smooth, efficient sentence or so demonstrating your ability to write?

TIP
Approach your logline step by step, and the process becomes less daunting.

Taming the Synopsis Beast

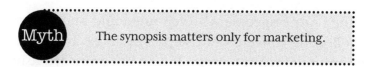

Myth   The synopsis matters only for marketing.

Start the synopsis early, and you'll not only revise more effectively but also be ready to market when the book is. Consider this. If the arcs of the minor characters clutter the synopsis, perhaps those tangents also weaken the novel? That's just one insight that a synopsis could reveal.

Condense these essentials into a single-spaced page:

◆ Inciting incident

◆ Central characters

◆ Setting

◆ Events intensifying the dilemma

◆ Events causing the climax

◆ Climax (Yes, you must admit how it ends.)

Many writers find the shift from writing fiction to briefly summarizing challenging. But a novelist who can focus the plot will land an agent or editor more easily. So persevere until the final product disguises any struggle. Because a persuasive synopsis needs:

● **Charm**.

Maintain your customary lyrical, suspenseful, or witty voice.

● **Clarity**.

Save the inference for your novel, not its condensation.

● **Causality**.

Reveal an inevitable yet surprising plot outcome.

Synopsis Dos and Don'ts

Don't:

Tell.

Complicate.

Oversimplify the antagonist.

Belabor minor details or events.

Ignore transitions.

Bury the climax.

Sound self-conscious or apologetic.

Do:

CAPITALIZE first mention of each character.

Use present tense.

Start with the inciting incident.

Emphasize *pressure points*.

Anchor plot with setting.

Animate verbs.

Seduce with your voice

TIP
Agents and editors are readers. The goal of the synopsis is to engage reader emotions.

Sample Logline/Synopsis

The Artists

Joan, who's lost her talent as a painter, believes a stranger can restore it. But what about her husband and children?

While sketching in the art section of a Manhattan bookstore, JOAN slips off her rings and lets a stranger take her to lunch. Her marriage is tepid, if not tenuous. TEDDY, her middle schooler, acts like a clinging hypochondriac, and his teenage sister, EMILY, behaves less like a juvenile than an actual delinquent.

ROD seduces with the art, passion, and emotion that Joan buried when responsibility overwhelmed her "hobby." She was never that talented, anyway. Right? But now she's a mother, wife, and art history professor without a soul.

Teaching, encouraging, and flirting, Rod manipulates his way into her life. He tantalizes. A splash of violet pastel resembles a caress. A flesh-colored blossom opens like a woman's lips. He even dismantles the walls that insulate Joan from memories of the best friend's death she accidentally caused decades earlier.

Frustrated by work, parenting, and her husband's demands for an intimacy she doesn't feel, Joan sneaks off to Rod's studio. Though painting together is still the only thing they share, her family notices that even when Joan's around, she isn't.

When, at husband MARTIN'S insistence, Joan invites Rod to dinner, the charming stranger encourages Martin to do some sneaking off himself. What about his wife's best friend? Didn't he hear that Martin dated the single, self-possessed, and elegant GRETCHEN before he met Joan? Joan's paintbrush isn't the only thing on fire. Gretchen and Martin succumb.

As Joan spends more and more time with Rod, she can't remember when she last felt this alive. She ignores the strained silences with her husband and her best friend. She ignores her kids, too, until Emily gets arrested at a pill party. Teddy, who won't admit he's being bullied, starts missing school. Joan can resist Rod no longer.

The next night, Teddy runs away. Joan bargains with God: "Bring back my son, and I'll never speak to Rod again."

In between conferences with the police, and on the verge of hiring a private detective, Joan tells Martin the truth, which elicits his confession. For their son's sake, they struggle to forgive each other.

The next morning, a bedraggled and ravenous Teddy sneaks back home. It's a chance for all of them to start over. When Martin reaches out to hug his son, his hand touches Joan's.

> **TIP**
> The synopsis abbreviates the story while maintaining its voice.

✔ **Checklist Exercise**: Brainstorming the Synopsis

Without looking at your manuscript, answer the questions below. Like a multiple choice test, your spontaneous first response is likely your best. Add any new discoveries to both synopsis and novel.

- ☐ How does the setting affect the plot?
- ☐ What initiates your protagonist's journey?
- ☐ What is your protagonist's most significant trait?
- ☐ What is your antagonist's most significant trait?
- ☐ What's at stake for your protagonist?
- ☐ Which three or four characters most affect your protagonist's arc?
- ☐ What are the *pressure points* of your novel?
- ☐ Which protagonist choices cause the climax?
- ☐ What or who makes your protagonist learn—and why? And what?

☞**Exercise**: Revising the Synopsis

Quickly draft a synopsis of your novel. Then rework it using the preceding "don't" and "do" lists. This could take a while. Isn't it worth it?

Demystifying the Query Letter

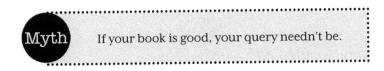

Myth If your book is good, your query needn't be.

If your query isn't good, how can an agent or editor know how good your book is? The query is an invitation, and different invitations attract different agents. Some value spunk; others prefer business-like neutrality. Some websites offer hints about the appropriate tone. But always aim to sound professional yet dynamic, while covering these basics:

● **Hook.**

Enticement to read on, e.g. personal contact, impressive endorsement, startling truth, edgy question, or special connection to this agent or agency.

● **Logline.**

Succinct commercial for your book.

● **Plot tease.**

Impetus to read the synopsis or first page.

● **Marketing plan.**

Compare your novel with successes in **current** publishing. How is your book different or better? What's your web presence and how will you use it to sell copies? Who are your contacts? What new ideas about sales will you bring to the table? What can you offer in terms of media, readings, conferences, speeches, and other opportunities? Really sell yourself and your book, but without promising anything you can't deliver.

● **Genre.**

Niche or publishing classification, i.e. mainstream, romance, cli fi, literary thriller, etc.

● **Platform.**

Personal assets, i.e. networks, **relevant** publications, credentials, expertise, contests, professional organizations, etc.

● **Word count.**

● **Closing.**

Thank you and any enclosures.

Begin your query with the hook and logline. In the next paragraph, summarize your plot. Then arrange or omit the other components to accentuate personal strengths, such as *concept*, contests, or connections.

Never *tell*, beg, or apologize. Rather than extolling your uniqueness or wit, seek that ambiguous line between bravado and modesty. Why wouldn't prospective agents love broad markets and big platforms? Use the confidence gained from drafting the log and synopsis to sound self-assured.

On the following page is an illustration of a query letter:

Kathy Sanguine
31 Crimson Terrace
Pewaukee, Wisconsin 53072

June 4, 2016

Dreamworks Literary Agency
911 Boardwalk Place Suite 66
New York, New York 10001

Dear Ms. Agentski,

Everyone loves dogs, especially heroic ones. In OUT FOR BLOOD, a severely depressed college student adopts a basset hound who must overcome a bite worse than a bark. The subject matter is apt for teens, mainstream readers, and anyone fond of dogs, romance, and happy endings.

The night Katie toys with killing herself, she decides a walk will help resolve things. In the dark she finds starving, freezing Bassie and impulsively sneaks him into her dorm. Although she moves out to raise him, his increasingly violent love nips frighten her. Dangerous as he might be, she can't survive without him: He's her only friend. On the night a prowler breaks into her apartment, Bassie saves Katie's life a second time. The new people she meets—particularly one reporter—give both Bassie and Katie another chance.

In 2014, I won first place in the "Writer's Digest" Short Fiction Contest and have published in "Story" and "Glimmer Train." I belong to the National Association of Women Writers and also Sisters in Crime. Broad Universe selected me to serve as a conference panelist, and I volunteer at Canine Companions, a national organization.

This novel (71,456 words) is ready for publication. Thank you in advance for considering it. May I send you a synopsis plus the first five pages?

Sincerely,

Kathy Sanguine

TIP
Marketing is assertive rather than hesitant or aggressive.

Exercise: Electrifying Your Query Letter

Few people enjoy bragging, especially on paper. To counteract this, applaud someone else first. Do you have a writing partner? Start there. Or write a query for an author you love. Just don't waste time researching anything but your own market. Feeling pepped? Type your query without stopping until you reach "thank you." Then tinker all you want, preferably when your novel pleases you.

Exercise: Starting the Agent/Publisher Search Sooner Than Later

It's never too early to identify the agents and agencies that delivered the books you love. Begin listing prospects so you're all set when your book is.

And so...

For deeper revision, assess your plot and theme as an agent or publisher would. As you complete the structural revision this inspires, articulate what excites you about this book. Your book! That's the route to exciting someone else.

Exploit this confidence to tackle the log, synopsis, and query. Better still, you've merged drafting, revising, and marketing into a unified process; you've integrated the tasks every novelist must complete in order to give readers the best experience possible.

Readers love suspense. So to be marketable, novels need momentum. In contrast, information, however essential, must move with sufficient charm and speed to seem barely visible. How do you accomplish that?

In the scene/summary system, drama balances the compressed time that launches the next event.

Imagine owning the tools to control time! Chapter four lets you do that. In your novel, anyway.

Deep Revision Tip
#4
Marketing necessities create revision opportunities.

The Scenic Route
Real versus Collapsed Time

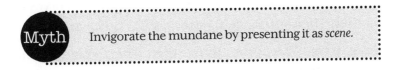

Myth   Invigorate the mundane by presenting it as *scene.*

If it's essential but unexciting, why slow it further? Fiction should be fun. We read it to watch someone else wallow in trouble; we read it to escape the pressure of time. In the real world, hours of pleasure feel like minutes, while discomfort and frustration often seem endless.

Unlike life, however, fiction creates the exquisite illusion of timelessness by maintaining the perfect pace.

⦿➤ Pace: The flow of information tempered by its expression.

Readers enjoy savoring the titillation of "the good parts" while zipping through whatever needs explaining, describing, or analyzing. Mundane material never needs live time.

⦿➤ Live Time: The sensation of cinematic immediacy—moment by moment.

Whether the novel's current time or a flashback, *live time* determines *scene.* But what if nothing intrigues during the moments between the antagonist kissing his wife goodbye at breakfast and kissing his mistress hello at lunch? That listless morning doesn't deserve full detail. Instead, use collapsed time.

> ✎ **TIP**
> Reserve *live time* for protagonist desperation—and reader desperation to watch.

⦿➤ Collapsed Time: Condensing hours, years, or even centuries into a few words or phrases.

Summary: A transition bridging or condensing the span between or within *real-time scenes.*

If you're shifting location, dispensing information, covering backstory, or transitioning within or between *scenes*, readers want you to pick up the pace. That means *summary*, and like *scene*, *summary* is independent of verb tense. Whether it happens to the characters now or occurred before, *summary* glides readers from past to present, moonlight to sunlight, or laughter to fury without dragging through the essential yet unsensational.

> ✏️
> **TIP**
> Control pace by shifting between the *live time* of *scene* and the *collapsed time* of *summary.*

To illustrate, Jan hears the buzzer, sets down the article she's completing for a medical journal, and opens her door to the guy who knocked her up on prom night twenty-two years earlier. Their interaction deserves the *live time* of *scene.*

What doesn't deserve that? Background. The high school encounter meant nothing to her; she struggled with abortion; he's searched for her ever since. Whatever precedes the drama of his unexpected appearance needs condensation. After that, she can open her arms to him, slam the door on his sandaled foot, or, under more dire circumstances, grab a gun.

Summary compresses and clarifies. Because it delves into either past or present, it can abbreviate or interpret every kind of detail, whether about the baby Jan gave up for adoption, or, in a different kind of novel, the whereabouts of Samuel the marine when his enemy appears.

But who wants *live time* for even hunky Sam adjusting water temperature, removing his clothes, and grabbing soap while bellowing "Oklahoma." Choose *summary* for the antagonist's stealthy entry, and *scene* for the attack on naked Sam as "the wind comes sweeping down the plain."

With *summary*, you can accelerate what readers know that the protagonist doesn't, or any form of character wonder, worry, or wistful recollection. *Summary* can fore-shadow, emphasize, track, reveal, and highlight the relationships between *scenes*, characters, description, and themes.

> ✏️
> **TIP**
> *Scene* dramatizes; *summary* speeds and synthesizes. The combination lets you control time.

Here's a well-known story illustrating how characters and narrator, *scene* and *summary* work in unison.

> When the pigs came of age, their mom sent them into the world, warning that shortcuts spell trouble. (*Summary*) Yet one piglet built his house of straw, while another used twigs. (*Summary*) Only the third brother heeded his mom and patiently constructed a brick dwelling. (*Summary*)
>
> Soon after the three homes went up, the Big Bad Wolf, undaunted by trichinosis, jogged to the straw house and sneered, "Let me in, or I'll huff and I'll puff and I'll blow your house in!" (*Scene*)
>
> "Not by the hair of my chinny chin chin," wailed the young hog. (*Scene*) But the vulpine exhaled a giant blast, and every sliver of straw fluttered away. (*Scene*) Licking his lips, the wolf gobbled the raw pork down to gnawed bones gleaming ivory in the fading light. (*Scene*)
>
> The outcome was identical at the second pig's house, except that smashed sticks enshrouded piglet bones. (*Summary*)
>
> Bricks, though, are as stout and sturdy as a hardworking porker. (*Summary*) Piglet #3 hummed a tune about impregnable walls, occasionally snickering at the exhaling and bellowing Volpone. (*Scene*) The white fur on the wolf's cheeks pinkened with exertion. (*Scene*) At last the exhausted wolf limped off, stomach growling as he foraged fruitlessly through the underbrush for something to nosh. (*Scene*) Every story has a moral, and so does this one. (*Summary*)

Like "The Three Little Pigs," every story fluctuates between the *live time* of *scene* and the *collapsed time* of *summary*. Kids adore repetition, but adults find it—repetitious. Let *summary* tighten anything redundant or inactive.

Though *scene* and *summary* support each other beautifully, readers still need a bridge for every change from *collapsed time to live*, or the reverse.

Memory is a strategic means of building that bridge, as is a sensation (such as perfume), an object (such as a cigarette lighter), or a gesture (such as yawning). Recollection and image are two viable techniques for easing readers from present to past or from ongoing action (daily) back to the present (now) or past (then).

Without a link between every shift, including past and present or external or internal, readers will experience a jolt. For them it doesn't blend beautifully the way it does for the author who conceived it and is both instinctively and purposefully aware of how everything meshes.

Since nothing is apparent to readers the way it is to the novelist, always glide from the remoteness of summary to the immediacy of current thought. Scenes bring the audience very close to the characters, and, however unconsciously, readers sense whether a narrator or character plays the starring role at ta particular moment.

Ideally, provide a transition each time you make any sort of shift. Most of these transitions, of course, will be quick, simple, and practically invisible.

Transition is the province of the narrator. That's partly because unlike real or fictitious people, the narrator knows how the story ends. This lets your narrator not only condense, but link, illuminate, describe, and inform.

TIP

Narrators control *summary*. Characters control *scene*.

Conflict, Complication, and Climax

Myth To bore readers is the worst "sin" a novelist can commit.

Though boredom is bad, confusion, repetition, or randomness often annoy even more. Novels need logical progression. Unfortunately, it's difficult for writers to evaluate the clarity of their own work; that's what feedback's for.

Feedback from astute readers is a first-rate revision aid. So is the ironically simple three-part structure you can apply globally to the entire scenario and, locally, to chapters, *scenes*, and, often, *summaries* or paragraphs.

Of course some lucky writers don't need to plan. Maybe they find it formulaic or constraining to repeat the set up, elaboration, and at least partial resolution. Still, most writers benefit from knowing where they're going, and all benefit from being able to evaluate structure—at every level of the novel. Isn't three-part structure a useful strategy to identify backtracking, paragraphs without beginning or end, and *scenes* that maintain the identical level of tension throughout?

There's a reason this pattern has survived for millennia. The movement from conflict to complication to climax encourages logical, credible, unified, and causal plotting. Tripartite structure accentuates how your novel's components mirror each other.

This classical structure helps you diagnose so you can repair. Having trouble with a chapter? Examine its progression from one source of trouble to another. Having trouble with a *scene*? Evaluate its starting point. Having trouble with a paragraph? Analyze its sequence.

This pattern promotes the causality that enhances *scene*, *summary*, and sometimes even sentence. An inciting incident launches the plot; a goal propels each *scene*, and some version of a topic sentence unifies paragraphs, whether *summary* or otherwise. All those English teachers were right. Imagine.

TIP

Capitalize on tradition to build paragraphs, *summaries*, *scenes*, and chapters.

The Sounds of Scene and Summary

Myth *Scenes* feel like fiction, while *summaries* seem dry as reports.

Why should any moment of your novel read like textbook? Both *summary* and *scene* must offer what's known as "voice."

The term "voice" literally means utterance of sound. Yet in the world of fiction, voice signals an almost magical quality: the illusion that a storyteller shares a secret adventure with a single reader. Doesn't every novelist want that?

Voice synthesizes the mutually influential components of detail and language. It's far easier to sizzle and sparkle with specifics, while generalities drift toward abstraction and cliché. Despite that, all novels also require the broad picture and the connecting links. Those mustn't sound as if they belong in a different book.

Most novelists experience at least some anxiety about *summary* sounding listless. Instead of continuing to worry, why not develop skill with being both efficient and lively? Concrete details invigorate word choice. To illustrate, replace "The unpleasant odor of his pet crazed him for months" with "Fido's flatulence made the small house barely habitable during winter."

> **TIP**
> Maintaining in the same voice in *summary* as in *scene* is easier than you think.

Beware, though, the unintentional humor of film tropes like flipping calendar pages, or an oak budding, browning, then sagging under snow. Clichés earned their reputation by losing their specificity long ago.

Once you develop proficiency with *summary,* you lessen the temptation to make everything a *scene.* If you stay in voice and select details thoughtfully, you can capture an entire event—or series of events—in a paragraph or even a single sentence. And do so in voice.

It's all about the language. To illustrate, picture the contrast between a tunnel and a window. Either generalities or over-used details plunge readers down a dark passageway. With nothing to visualize or even imagine, it's dull and certainly uninviting. On the other hand, imagery flings open a window, changing the view and admitting sound and fragrance.

> **TIP**
> Let the light in.

Inference

Language and imagery play off each other. If there's nothing to see, the word choice will reflect that. Certainly literal imagery can compel. But because it has only one level of meaning, it sometimes lacks depth.

That's where symbolism comes in. Careful, though. Once you introduce this additional layer, you must handle the literal component, which is usually physical, meticulously. If you don't, the sun might rise as a bright copper penny, only to melt like a pat of butter when the day ends. Accuracy (no one burrows into the sky) and consistency (if you begin with "burrow," don't switch to "wade") lets readers infer what you want them to.

Inference comes easily to most fiction readers, because humans are hard-wired to seek patterns and draw conclusions. This ability is instinctive.

Now. Does the figure above resemble three random lines, or an imperfect triangle? You probably filled in the empty spaces, almost as if nothing was missing.

Fiction works the same way. The more you trust readers to complete the incomplete without your nudging, the more they can reach their own conclusions. And the more they'll enjoy your novel.

One path to inference is double-duty details.

Double-Duty Detail: Image simultaneously accomplishing more than one task.

Maybe Wilhelmina leaves the suitcase with all her possessions on the train transporting her from Hometown, USA to Big City. Accidentally, of course. What does the missing baggage reveal about the protagonist and her future plans? In addition to describing, double-duty details foreshadow, tease, dispense irony, add tension, develop character, create mood, and so on.

Choose details that imply a cause/effect connection, and you'll be less inclined to clutter or repeat. Since excessive detail obscures what you want readers to notice, choose a few terrific details and then streamline. Let readers infer the rest.

Exercise: Deepening Detail

Choose a paragraph from your novel and make its detail more specific, concrete, and symbolic. Initially, this could feel challenging. You might even get frustrated. Don't give up! You can train yourself to substitute imagery for abstraction and double-duty details for literal ones. The more often you try, the easier it becomes. Apply the techniques you discover reworking this paragraph to the rest of your novel.

TIP

Readers want to read without constant intrusion from the novelist.

Solidifying Your Scenes

Some of the *scenes* that are the easiest to write are the ones that readers like least. If your characters are serving lasagna, no matter how much you want to share its preparation, don't. Your readers want neither cooking lessons nor omission of the *scene* they've wanted to read since starting the book. If your characters have flirted for 300 pages, when they finally make love, let the couple—and those reading about them—savor it. In scene.

But if neither pasta nor sex is involved, how do you decide whether readers want *scene* or *summary*? One question is whether this time period develops arc, propelling the protagonist toward the climax. Another question is whether there's a clear goal for one or more characters in the *scene*.

●❖ **Scene Goal**: Intense, explicit character desire that impels choice and action.

Since characters propel novels, only character goals count. Scene goals aren't about a writer's need to introduce the protagonist's neighbor, develop the symbolism, or any other author concern.

To illustrate, the scene goals below thrust a familiar story to its inevitable conclusion:

● **Goal:** Antagonist wants to eliminate any competition for "the fairest of them all."

● **Goal:** Snow White wants to escape beheading.

● **Goal:** Dwarves want to wake the lovely sleeping maiden.

● **Goal:** Snow White wants her prince to come.

● **Goal:** Antagonist wants protagonist to eat the poisonous apple.

● **Goal:** Handsome prince wants to wake the lovely sleeping maiden.

Scene goals help you avoid starting too soon or late. Notice that various characters can drive scene goals, but every goal affects the protagonist. To meet your own goal of tension on every page, plan a goal for every *scene*.

↪ **Exercise**: Pacing with Scene Goals

Identify the goal for each *scene* in your novel. Use your discoveries to sharpen *scenes* and decide if any would read better as *summary*. Revise as needed.

TIP

Unless you have a viable scene goal, choose *summary* instead.

Setting: the Backdrop for the Action

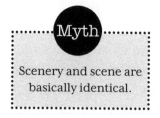

Not at all. *Scenes* have goals and drama, while setting rarely does more than support the plot. Of course at the *scene* opening, readers want to know where, when, and what's at stake. Once the predicament is grounded, though, readers prefer entering action already underway.

Detailed description of setting or anything else usually interferes with the swift buildup of momentum. Does the setting intensify connection with the characters, or just languish? Most writers can rapidly generate room dimensions, travel itineraries, and grocery lists, although such details squelch reader interest at even greater velocity. It matters that Mira's escape route vanishes when the sun sets. But her changing the van's oil? No one cares unless it's mixed with someone's blood.

Elmore Leonard famously warned against writing the parts readers won't read. Those routine details that flood so easily from writer's minds drown readers in logistical overkill.

●✧ **Logistical Overkill**: Painstaking delineation of the obvious or insignificant.

Replace *logistical overkill* with unique imagery or understated symbolism. This means that sunshine never smiles and nights have ceased to be dark and stormy.

At its best, setting enhances conflict and theme. In David Guterson's *Snow Falling on Cedars*, for instance, the gnarled tree limbs cradling the young lovers also represent the conventions that will eventually strangle. When an ordinary setting becomes extraordinary, you've created the sense of place readers expect.

In every instance, though, setting must serve plot and characterization—not the other way around. Think about setting as creating characters rather than merely surrounding them. No one escapes the influence of where we grew up, where we put down roots. Characters are equally influenced. How does environment affect who they are? Why is this location unlike any other? What would change if this event occurred elsewhere?

When setting contributes to plot, you cement causality. It's no accident that she threatens divorce in the barn where they first kissed. Use setting to make meaning. If the protagonist and would-be suitor keep rowing out to the middle of the lake, both characters and readers must experience some change every time the boat anchors there.

Exercise: Capitalizing on Setting

Instead of just deleting *logistical overkill*, consider how this information could potentially intrigue. For example, what do the ingredients in Ed's pantry reveal about his personality? Find the *logistical overkill* in your book and try to transform it. If you can't, delete it.

The Hook

Novelists often open *scenes* by grounding. Although readers need that, they want instant drama, mystery, humor, or surprise even more. Psychologically, context isn't the impetus that mobilizes, gets things underway, builds suspense, and summons emotion.

Causality underlies many hooks, because preceding events thrust characters into the conflict impelling the next *scene* or chapter.

Perhaps, you wonder, is offering that stimulation over and over repetitive and boring? About as boring as the threat of continuous excitement or pleasure.

Naturally you want to vary pacing, because exhilaration lessens if it never fluctuates. But is the opening of a *scene* or chapter really the place to eliminate conflict? Journalists are absolutely right: lead with a hook. Pretty much every time.

Besides, the opening sets up the *scene* for the writer as well as the reader. What's at stake here? Where is this going? What thrusts both plot and protagonist forward? Use such questions to tantalize at the start of every *scene*. Ideally, in its first sentence.

Too often, the real hook gets buried two or three or five sentences into the *scene* or chapter. But why make readers wait to discover what's at stake right now? Don't hoard your hooks.

Don't neglect the closing hook, either. Only your final *scene* can thrive without it. Always suggest that, yes, this *scene* changed the protagonist, but there's plenty of trouble ahead. Bad trouble. Reassure that things won't end well until—"The End."

> **TIP**
> Opening and ending hooks affect the quality and momentum of every *scene*.

Can't find a hook? You're starting the *scene* too early or late, aren't sure where it's going, or putting in *scene* what should be *summary*.

Once you decide if this material warrants a *scene* and where it starts, the following parameters can help:

Usually Successful Hooks	**Usually Unsuccessful Hooks**
Pressure point	Mundane setting
Action or decision	Excessive description
Threat	Status quo
Secret	Repetition of recent events
Passion	Disembodied dialogue
Surprise	Backstory
Obstacle	Rumination
Irony	Cliché
Question	Superficial generalization
Ticking clock	*Logistical overkill*
Foreshadowing	Stereotype or trope
Humor	Backtracking
Super-short sentence	Long, clumsy sentence
Vigorous or lyrical language	Vagueness or abstraction

↪**Exercise**: Hooking Them In

Check for a hook at both ends of every *scene* in your novel. Add or repair as needed. The bonus? This also double-checks whether any *scene* would work better as *summary*.

TIP
Start and end every scene but the last with a hook

Seventeen Ways to Screw up a *Scene*

Your readers will love you if you revise to correct these issues.

1. Omit opening and ending hooks. (No propulsion.)

2. Ignore the traditional pattern of conflict, complication, climax. (No causality.)

3. Include too many characters. (Busy.)

4. Focus on rumination and decision-making instead of action. (Static.)

5. Rely on coincidence. (Improbable.)

6. Disregard character goals. (Aimless.)

7. Summarize suspense. (Frustrating.)

8. Imbalance power. (Oversimplified.)

9. Ignore the external world. (Abstract.)

10. Concentrate exclusively on the visual. (Incomplete.)

11. Dump large gobs of unbelievable dialogue. (Tedious.)

12. Resolve before the end. (Anti-climactic.)

13. Teach your audience about information, ideas, or themes. (Condescending.)

14. Disobey the laws of physics. (Counter-intuitive.)

15. Disobey the laws of the heart. (Cynical.)

16. Break every writing rule you ever heard. (Disastrous.)

17. Follow every writing rule you ever heard. (Disastrous.)

TIP
Build scenes from character growth and the cost of missed opportunity.

✔ **Checklist Exercise**: Establishing *Scene*

- ☐ Does every *scene* in your book have a goal?

- ☐ Does every *scene* except the last begin and end with a hook?

- ☐ Do you start when the conflict does?

- ☐ Does scenery support plot?

- ☐ Is your protagonist appealing and plucky?

- ☐ Is your antagonist multi-faceted and credible?

- ☐ Do you focus at least as much on what characters do as what they think about?

- ☐ Do your *scenes* withhold information and promise upcoming secrets?

Dialogue: The Dance

Real conversation can be really boring. Terrible dialogue is terribly easy to write and thus terribly tantalizing to writers, though not to readers. The alternative? Pretext, subtext, and context.

● **Pretext.**

Dialogue can spew forth like a faucet with a broken shut-off valve. Just like *scene*, dialogue requires motivation and momentum rather than simply a break from narration or a misguided attempt to supply exposition.

Not: "How are you today, on your December 29th birthday, here in Montreal?"

"Not so very good just now. How are you?"

But: "You could've mentioned that before all these people drove through the snow for your birthday."

"Really. What would you have done instead?"

TIP
Use dialogue to reveal motivation.

● **Subtext.**

Direct speech not only *tells* but strains credibility, since people often postpone confrontation by insinuating until the moment of explosion. Dialogue benefits from subtext, or the implicit meaning underlying what characters never vocalize. Let readers infer who won the argument. Is it the character not actually accusing, or the character not actually hearing the implicit accusation?

Not: "That's unacceptable, Marci. Absolutely ridiculous. You can't go to my mother's funeral in that get up. I don't want you embarrassing me, especially today. Now go change."

But: Marci's mother bit her lip. "You're wearing that to my mother's funeral?"

TIP
Strengthen dialogue with the words no character ever speaks.

● **Context.**

No one wants to wonder who said what. Or to see "said" over and over. Writers might wish otherwise, but "said" reads exactly like any other word. Clarify where the characters are and what they're doing; this reduces abstraction and eliminates the reader struggling to track who's talking.

Not: "I don't know how we'll resolve this."

"You always say that."

"This time it's different."

But: Patsy glared down at the linoleum. "I don't know how we'll resolve this."

"You always say that."

She slid her wedding ring past her knuckle. "This time it's different."

TIP
Stage business can identify speaker and clarify subtext.

Vary the techniques used for speaker attribution, and avoid distracting synonyms for "said."

Not: "How dare you talk to my daughter that way," Terri harassed.

"She's also my daughter," her husband coughed. "My daughter, too," Frank grimaced.

But: "How dare you talk to my daughter that way?"

"She's also my daughter." Frank looked away. "My daughter."

TIP
Motivate, insinuate, and substantiate your dialogue.

∽**Exercise**: Adding Physicality to Dialogue

Subtly observe conversations in public places. What do people look at? How do they gesture and use objects? Note facial expressions. Develop a list and keep it handy.

More Dialogue about Dialogue

Good dialogue lets readers eavesdrop while offering:

1. Credibility.

Speech or gesture must respond to something said, seen, or heard.

Not: Kent sneezed. "Let's wait till tomorrow,"

But: Kent eyed the clock. "Let's wait till tomorrow."

2. Momentum.

Propel the plot with what the characters never express aloud.

Not: "I'm starting to think that if neither one of us is willing to change that maybe we can't go on like this any longer. Does it seem that way to you?"

But: "Enough." Nora walked out without looking back.

3. Correctness.

Periods and commas fall inside quotation marks, and stage business requires a separate sentence.

Not: "Let's call it a night", Louella barely covered her yawn, "I've had it".
"Already"?, Bob held her eyes until she looked away.

But: "Let's call it a night." Louella barely covered her yawn. "I've had it."
"Already?" Bob held her eyes until she looked away.

TIP
Good dialogue titillates like the Tango and bites like the Tarantella.

✔ **Checklist Exercise:** Dramatizing Dialogue

☐ Does your dialogue always have a pretext?

☐ Do you support dialogue with context?

☐ Does your subtext escalate to a confrontation?

☐ Are exchanges brief?

☐ Does your dialogue express only what a character can realistically say?

☐ Do you alternate between "said" and stage business or viable synonyms?

☐ Are periods, commas, and question marks where they belong?

Summing up the *Summary*

Yes, *summary* is harder to write than *scene*, but since each has a job to do, you need to master both. *Scene* offers drama, while *summary* efficiently dispenses the context needed to appreciate that drama. Rumination—especially in *live time*—rarely adds. Why not speed introspection with *summary?* At their best, *summaries* invigorate *scenes* by condensing what readers need to know.

How to Strand Readers in the Middle of a Lake in a Boat without Oars

● Omit the grounding of who, what, where, when, why.

● Ignore the causal relationships between events.

● Jump-cut each time you change *scene*.

● Exclude any emotion too complex for characters to articulate.

● Frequently alter time and location, always without transition.

● Frequently switch between psychological and physical detail, always without transition.

Instead? Use *summary* to ground and support *scenes*.

The Roles of *Summary*

In combination with *scene*, *summary* creates the illusion of timelessness by providing:

1. Compression.

Abbreviate the set-up for the upcoming pay-off:

> The angel rescued a boy from drowning, banished locusts from a Kansas farm, and destroyed a man's love-letter to his girlfriend before his wife found it. But the angel couldn't rescue himself from the nondescript, married elementary school teacher he loved more than immortality.

TIP
Only real tension deserves *live time.*

2. Transition.

Innovatively shift time or place, perhaps with a symbol, lyric, or allusion.

> "Bye, bye blackbird," Ginger decided, and without consulting a soul, resigned from Microsoft and reserved a Hong Kong flight and hotel for her fresh start.

TIP
Use concrete specifics to transport not just characters, but readers from one place to another.

3. Context.

Thicken plot with secrets, clues, even a smidgen of backstory.

> Mayor Billings Swift Jr.'s Vermont town lacked the mystique of nearby Hell's Gate or St. George. But tiny North Hero had its own version of dragons, and the proud, twenty-six-year-old junior college graduate braced himself to confront one.

TIP
Intensify suspense with innuendo.

4. Explanation.

Weave information into plot and characterization.

> Thoth, the ibis-headed Egyptian god, invented writing, and Steve revered him for bestowing the only wisdom of any value.

TIP
Educate almost invisibly.

5. Propulsion.

End every *scene* except the last by launching the next.

> Beethoven recoiled from the shout as though slapped. The ringing would follow, pulsating through his chest and torso as the notes slipped from his grasp. To complete the Third Piano Concerto, he must abandon his Vienna home. Heiligenstadt would provide the silence where the music hid. It had to.

TIP
Summary can lure and synthesize by hooking at both ends of each *scene*.

When you accentuate, promise, or warn with *summary*, design still matters. Consider the loveliest necklaces. They transform heaps of precious stones into creations that connect each piece securely, exquisitely, and gracefully. Omit the knots that stabilize the jewels—that mark each gem as both individual and part of a whole—and the work feels incomplete. *Scene* and *summary* must mesh the same way.

On the other hand, who wants to see distracting fasteners in either a necklace or novel? The trick is making *summary* glitter while it sets off the *scenes* it supports.

TIP
Neither *scene* nor *summary* is inherently superior. Readers need both.

Seasoning Your *Summaries*

Many writers worry that everything out of scene will bore, that it won't "feel like a novel." To fix this, omit *logistical overkill* and match the voice of the *summary* to the character interaction within the *scene* itself.

When it comes to summary, many writers focus more on rushing than stimulating. But who ever said that *summary* can only use denotation?

Denotation: Literal, objective wording.

Write your *summary* like a denotative report, and it will sound like this:

> He stepped about four and a half feet back from the mirror in the largest bathroom to enter the walk-in closet and select attire for a busy morning, restaurant lunch, and evening out. He wanted garments that reflected his occupation and activities.

Specifics provide personality and spunk. This is especially true when you add connotation.

●◆ **Connotation**: Language with emotional, cultural, historical, and often symbolic associations.

The tepid passage above is a lame paraphrase of the compelling opening that launches Peter Mayle's *The Vintage Caper*. The energetic original illustrates that *summary* can—and should—appeal as much as any other sentence in your novel.

In Mayle's version, nothing happens during the first few lines: the guy gets up and prepares to leave for work. Yet despite that, voice, sleek sentence structure, and vibrant detail dramatize. In just a few sentences, readers already know tons about this character and can't wait to know more. This introduction sings like a *scene*.

The best *summaries* blend invisibly with the scenes they support.

Spice for the *Summary*

● **Causality.**

Hint how offstage events will trigger the next *scene*. Readers don't need to watch Mortimer choose a wig—only to know that it doesn't quite fit, making it extremely precarious.

● **Emotion.**

Move time not only chronologically, but psychologically. An allusion to summer won't engage readers like "humidity that smothers and soaks."

● **Cinema.**

Evoke the concrete sensations of lilacs or rap music. *Summary* need not be abstract.

● **Unity.**

Echo your motifs, like the personal, economic, political, and social versions of imbalance in Jonathan Franzen's *The Corrections*.

● **Mystery.**

Withhold. What ailment, unmentionable in polite company, do all Greendale inhabitants suffer? A good novel is a puzzle. Help readers work it.

● **Charm.**

Disguise exposition, fact, or backstory with a welcoming tone. The way to get plenty of drama live time is to stay in voice. Tread the fine line between drab and distracting detail and between lagging versus rushing too much. Why not watch for illustrations of successful summaries in the novel you read. Maybe even jot down the best examples?

Obviously, understated wording works as well in *summary* as in everything else. And staying in voice doesn't mean cluttering or overdoing. If summary sometimes lacks flavor, heavy-handed wording smothers like an overdose of Tabasco sauce. The goal is balance: between *scene* and *summary*, denotation and connotation, implication and description.

As you develop greater confidence in your *summaries*, you'll choose *scene* or *summary* based exclusively on the inherent drama of the material.

Welcome Aspects of *Summary*	Troublesome Aspects of *Summary*
Efficiency	Haste
Causality	Lengthy or irrelevant backstory
Originality	Professorial tone
Pertinent facts or ideas	*Logistical overkill*
Interpretation	Lack of momentum
Foreshadowing	Spelling out
Imagery	Abstraction
Symbolism	Generalities
Humor	*Telling* what you can *show*
Lyricism	Sentimentality

TIP
Offer readers an equally appealing voice in *scene* and *summary*.

꘏**Exercise**: Energizing the *Summary*

List your strengths as a novelist, i.e. imagery, humor, rhythm—whatever you love about your writing when you feel good about it. Perhaps such a list makes you slightly uncomfortable? Work through that, possibly with a fellow writer. Assessing your talents is a valuable strategy not only for improving *summaries* but also for revising and marketing.

Have your list ready? Now choose a *scene* from your novel that would work better as a *summary* and create a version that's both efficient and entertaining. The first time this could be time-consuming. Persevere without perseverating. Remind yourself that the person writing your *summaries* is the same one who writes your *scenes*. Consciously utilize the writing attributes from that list.

Patience will produce discoveries that you can apply to every *summary* in your novel—and perhaps to other issues, as well.

And so...

Characters dominate *scenes*; narrators dominate *summaries*. But the entire novel must hold together. Some force must unify action and insight, *scene* and *summary*, *live time* versus *collapsed*.

What's that force? Your narrator, who originates the unity and context that no character can credibly provide. Despite the narrator's major impact, readers notice this crucial role mainly when it's intrusive or absent, much the way baseball fans notice the umpire only when they dispute a pitch or strike. Neither game nor novel works unless both umpire and narrator get it right.

Point of view comes from the type of narrator the author chooses. But whether broad or narrow, every point of view has limitations, because either limited or limitless has certain drawbacks. Successful narrators compensate for those by offering entertainment, guidance, foreshadowing, and synthesis.

That's enough responsibility to deserve your full attention. So the upcoming chapter focuses on the kingdom of the narrator: point of view.

Deep Revision Tip
#5
Revise by alternating between big picture and individual sentence.

6

Point of View

Power and Politics

Myth   Point of view is an esoteric subject relevant only to literary novelists.

Everyone defines plot pretty much the same way. Point of view, on the other hand, is far more elusive, though equally critical. Many novelists ignore it altogether, or reduce it to what the narrator can or can't legitimately reveal.

While violations irritate, that's a small fraction of the narrator's influence. Point of view can escalate tension, sharpen focus, deepen characterization, and emphasize theme. Aren't these issues relevant to every novelist in every genre?

Whether your narrator exalts a talking cat or satirizes the owner of twenty-one Siamese, those seemingly trivial pronouns determine the reader's relationship to your characters. After all, the narrator controls breadth, trustworthiness, and degree of detachment.

The sensation of intimacy originates in narrator proximity to the protagonist. Beyond that, the width of the window into the story dictates what seems to happen, and—what that seems to mean. Point of view releases and shapes story, opening certain possibilities and restricting others. Whatever the genre, the narrator affects the interpretation of reality and truth within that particular fictional world.

TIP
The story is inseparable from its teller.

Point of View 101

Narrator breadth ranges from narrow subjectivity to far-flung access stretching anywhere and revealing anyone. Here's the breakdown:

First Person: "I"

Example: I smelled the corpse before I saw it.

In first person, character and narrator are two facets of one individual: the character lives the story; the narrator delivers it. However, the narrator and character can't sound like two different people, because—they're not.

Still, their roles differentiate them. Characters live in the present and recall the past, while the narrator exists outside time. For the narrator, even the ending has already happened.

In standard first person, the narrator guides in *summary* and within *scene*, while the character speaks, thinks, and acts.

But if the entire novel captures a character looking back on the past, this adds another narrator: one represents the younger perspective, another assumes the older. *Great Expectations*, by Charles Dickens, illustrates retrospective point of view, with Pip recounting the story of his childhood.

❦ First Person Retrospective: Narrator interpreting events the character previously experienced.

Example: I smelled the corpse before I saw it. The stench engulfed me, as it had when my three-year-old fingers clutched Mommy's icy hand.

A retrospective narrator observes differently than a conventional one. The classic examples of this perspective are Charles Dickens' *Great Expectations* and Harper Lee's *To Kill a Mockingbird*.

In either novel, the voice of the adult narrator looking back is absolutely distinct from the narrator who illuminates character behavior during the *scenes* covering childhood. Although the juvenile and adult narrators must never appear to clash, they still differ in terms of perception, sophistication, word choice, and sentence structure.

Retrospective or not, first person distinguishes the struggling protagonist from the discerning narrator. This disparity can evoke dramatic irony, or readers inferring what the character doesn't.

First-person narrators build worlds by inhabiting them, assessing them, or both. Nick Carraway of *The Great Gatsby*, for example, participates in the plot while largely remaining remote from it. He informs us, with self-righteous and possibly dubious honesty, that he's never deceitful and thus not susceptible to the immorality of Gatsby's world.

Nick's perspective, though potentially ironic, contrasts with the glitz, gangsters, and grip of the past. In Fitzgerald's novel, its narrator provides the moral center, though narrators need not necessarily assume that role.

First Person Overview

Possible Difficulties: Explaining, complaining, or subjectivity, along with conveying physical appearance, other characters' thoughts, and events with the point-of-view character absent.

Assets: Intimacy. Freedom to glide between the protagonist actions and thoughts.

Second Person: "You"

Example: You smelled the corpse before you saw it.

This perspective plants readers in the novel's world along with the characters. So it can feel even more immediate than first person. To illustrate, the opening of Jay McInerney's *Bright Lights, Big City* deposits its audience in some sort of strange club with some sort of strange p   . The reader is right there—weirdness, drugs, and all. While this can feel electric and exciting, second person isn't an easy point of view to maintain.

Second Person Overview

Possible Difficulties: If the view from the edge exhilarates, from there it's easy to fall. This unconventional stance can threaten suspension of disbelief by reminding readers that they're reading.

Assets: Intimacy, originality, electricity.

Third Person: "He," "She," or "It"

Third-person narration ranges in breadth from one individual perspective to all-encompassing.

Third Person Limited

●❖ **Third Person Limited**: Restricted to a single "he," "she," or "it" vantage point.

Example: Eloise smelled the corpse before she saw it.

Third limited offers first-person advantages—and concerns—from farther off. This perspective excels at irony. You might imagine the narrator positioned just behind the character, offering a slightly different slant, often humorous in nature, on the character's own version of self and world.

In the opening of Rick Moody's *The Diviners*, for instance, the character complains of pain in the head, the feet, and just about every part of her body. Self-pity at this level might prove difficult for readers to endure.

So Moody provides contrast. The narrator's hyperbolic exaggeration of the character's trials and tribulations elevates her trivial miseries to the agony a flayed saint might endure. The result is a fun read.

The differentiated voices of character and narrator reveal foibles, introduce humor, and in this instance make the hypochondria easier to bear. Finally, the narrator/character distinction reminds readers that Rosa Elisabetta Meandro might not be the only one taking herself too seriously. At its best, point of view raises questions about perception, self-image, and thus truth itself.

Third Person Limited Overview

Possible Difficulties: The thoughts of other characters, over-active narrator, and scenes without the point-of-view character.

Assets: Irony, intimacy balanced with distance and objectivity, and narrator/character contrast.

Third Person Omniscient

●◆ **Third Person Omniscient**: Broadened to go everywhere and perceive everything.

Example: Who can say how many corpses decomposed under this soil?

In omniscient, voice is crucial, because in this point of view the narrator leads the cast. Since omniscient highlights narrator or setting, it works particularly well for fantasy and historical fiction.

Consider the opening of *The Dispossessed*, by Ursula LeGuin. The entry point into this novel is a wall. It's described in minute detail. The barrier protecting Anarres has outlived many generations of people, any of whom could've climbed it. The significance of this wall isn't the feeble physical structure that isolates this world. What matters? The unexpected attitude toward isolation.

Normally, people view walls as keeping something out. In LeGuin's novel, though, the narrator's dispassionate voice enhances a vast irony: supposedly, this barrier leaves the Port of Anarres "free"—protected from the rest of the world rather than cut off from it. Omniscient point of view is a perfect match for the themes here.

If the scope of your novel is broad—such as the plight of a world, an empire, or several generations, omniscient might be the best strategy for what you hope to accomplish.

Third Person Omniscient Overview

Possible Difficulties: Remoteness, transitions, tendency to teach or preach, and complex structure.

Assets: Freedom to penetrate any location or character mind, at any place or time.

Roving: Shifts Between Two or More Character Perspectives

The roving perspective can occur in first person, third, or sometimes both. It offers intimacy while eliminating the restriction to a single character.

First Person Roving ("I"):

Example: Gal: On my highest heels, I teetered toward a corpse I smelled before I saw it.

Example: Guy: I kinda figured I'd smell the goon's corpse before I saw it.

Example: Pup: Even at three months, of course I smelled the corpse before I saw it.

Third Person Roving ("he," "she," "it"):

Example: Lulabelle smelled the corpse before she saw it.

Example: Big Moe smelled the corpse before he saw it.

Example: Little Rover smelled the corpse before he saw it.

Novels customarily rove in either first person or third. But it's possible to use both. *Before and After*, for example, by Rosellen Brown, presents the father's perspective in first person but uses third person for the other point of view characters.

Roving Overview

Possible Difficulties: Transitions, distinct voice for every character, and complex structure.

Assets: Intimacy plus breadth.

Managing Point of View

One might sub-divide the basic point of view possibilities further. But classification matters far less than consistency. More important still, know what your point of view offers—and doesn't—so you can revise accordingly. That lets you capitalize on point of view's greatest asset: using the narrator's perspective to influence the reader's.

TIP
The narrator's stance controls reader response to the protagonist's journey.

Narrator Positions Contrasted

● First Person

Assets	Possible Difficulties
Empathy	Narrow scope
Irony	Excessive intrusion
Intimacy	Cumbersome description

TIP
Compensate by balancing commentary with behavior, action, and setting.

TIP
Compensate by capitalizing on readers experiencing the *scene* as it occurs.

● Second Person

Assets	Possible Difficulties
Intimacy	Inconsistency
Edginess	Artificiality
Unconventionality	Unconventionality

● Third Limited

Assets	Possible Difficulties
Dual vision	Excessive intrusion
Intimacy + distance	Narrow Scope
Irony	Access to other characters

TIP
Compensate by contrasting what the narrator knows that the protagonist doesn't.

- Omniscient

Assets	Possible Difficulties
Breadth	Lack of intimacy
Physicality	Transitions
Clairvoyance	Excessive intrusion

TIP
Compensate with a wise, alluring narrator.

- Roving

TIP
Compensate with distinct voices and sleek shifts between perspectives.

Assets	Possible Difficulties
Breadth	Blurring of voices
Intimacy	Transitions
Clairvoyance	Complex Structure

Point of View Tricks and Tribulations

Myth There's a perfect point of view for every novel.

Point of view is the window controlling what your readers see. Whether you choose one that's wide open or barely so, you'll encounter both possibilities and problems. First person lacks distance, while omniscient seems remote.

Whichever point of view you select, your readers swiftly develop unconscious expectations about what the narrator can reasonably know or express. Violate those assumptions, and you betray trust in the storyteller. And, for better or worse, point of view depends on the beholder perception. Whatever feels like a violation is one, whether it's technically legal or not. And vice versa.

TIP
Revision is incomplete until you assess narrator as well as narrative.

Obviously, no novelist disappoints readers intentionally. But while adding details or hinting themes, authors sometimes blur the narrator's identity. For example, a first person narrator can't credibly report, "I shook out my glorious mane of lustrous hair." Instead, she might say, "Removing a long blonde strand from my black sweater, I resumed applying Bountiful Bouquets nail polish." This distinction is subtle but crucial, and in fact most point of view violations are more insidious than blatantly extolling one's own tresses.

But credible observations and consistent pronouns are just the foundation. To dazzle, point of view must shape a novel's world in a way that reveals our own. To illustrate that, consider how Todd reached the conclusion below.

> Todd quit sauntering the instant he knew Roger prepared to attack.

Incredulous readers want to know how Todd "knows." Still, it's distracting to scrupulously differentiate knowledge from suspicion each time. Instead, exploit the human capacity to deduce:

> The silence told Todd that Roger prepared to attack.

Or

> When Roger's smile vanished, Todd knew his opponent prepared to attack.

Or

> Familiar with Roger's moods, Todd could predict the moment of explosion.

In either life or fiction, concrete details and past history produce plausible speculation. To texture your fiction with this subtle technique, use the hard-wired human survival skill of faux clairvoyance.

●◆ **Faux Clairvoyance**: Inference based on physical or psychological evidence that permits expanding point of view without overtly violating it.

External clues like squinting, facial expressions, and posture let both characters and readers conjecture, and, done properly, it won't feel like a point of view violation. *Faux clairvoyance* adds concreteness and a bit of mystery while eliminating the need for cumbersome, distancing words like "wondered," "speculated," "supposed," "imagined," and so on.

Similarly, if you introduce one character through another, you can raise questions while revealing both.

Readers first glimpse this protagonist through the eyes of a man who's equally determined to marry for money:

If she had appeared to be catching a train, he might have inferred that he had come on her in the act of transition between one and another of the country-houses which disputed her presence after the close of the Newport season; but her desultory air perplexed him. She stood apart from the crowd, letting it drift by her to the platform or the street, and wearing an air of irresolution which might, as he surmised, be the mask of a very definite purpose. It struck him at once that she was waiting for some one, but he hardly knew why the idea arrested him. —Edith Wharton, *The House of Mirth*

How can he possibly know whether Lily's waiting for someone? His inference works because readers discover the basis for his assumptions: "irresolution" and "her desultory air." This adds suspense. Are the spectator's conclusions accurate? Indirect characterization escalates tension more subtly than overt drama, because, in a sense, it's another form of subtext.

Shortly after this initial encounter, Wharton establishes the protagonist's anxiety about being seen leaving a man's apartment. They only talked! Still, if anyone noticed her, she'd be devalued on the marriage market. The *faux clairvoyance* of this next passage slyly captures Lily's distress:

There was no one in sight, however, but a char-woman who was scrubbing the stairs. Her own stout person and its surrounding implements took up so much room that Lily, to pass her, had to gather up her skirts and brush against the wall. As she did so, the woman paused in her work and looked up curiously, resting her clenched red fists on the wet cloth she had just drawn from her pail. She had a broad sallow face, slightly pitted with small-pox, and thin straw-coloured hair through which her scalp shone unpleasantly.

"I beg your pardon," said Lily, intending by her politeness to convey a criticism of the other's manner.

The woman, without answering, pushed her pail aside, and continued to stare as Miss Bart swept by with a murmur of silken linings. Lily felt herself flushing under the look. What did the creature suppose? Could one never do the simplest, the most harmless thing, without subjecting one's self to some odious conjecture? —Edith Wharton, *The House of Mirth*

Anxiety magnifies Lily's contempt. Her snobbishness, though, foreshadows her own doom, because this novel will trace her descent to the level of the woman she calls "creature." The foreshadowing is understated, and the omission of "Lily wondered what the woman thought" introduces pleasurable ambiguity. Does the char-woman stare suspiciously, or merely quit scrubbing? What exactly does Lily know? What do her judgments reveal about who she is and what she wants?

Like *faux clairvoyance*, unreliable narration invites reader participation. Narrators who consistently misjudge, often to their own benefit, are considered unreliable. This is another technique for engaging readers, who can contrast the description with the conclusions drawn from it.

In *The Emperor's Children*, the central character is an author named Murray Thwaite. At one point he ruminates on what he considers student enthusiasm over his guest presentation. His self-assessment is as hilarious as it is painful. He attacks the shallowness of the audience while ignoring his own. Delusions of grandeur convince him that everyone has listened attentively, even while he dismissively wonders what the heck these simpletons think about. Claire Messud's indictment of this character is subtle but incriminating and all the more amusing because it's understated.

Thwaite sees only what he wants to, and clues from the narrator help readers discern this. Three hours. Isn't that an awfully long time to talk without a break? Sadly, the host—not the speaker—eyes the clock. The faulty judgments mount. Why accuse students of babbling thoughtlessly without overhearing what they say? Finally, both Thwaite's audience and Messud's identify the listless applause as anything but appreciative or sincere.

Point of view offers an opportunity to question what is "true." Unreliable narrators mimic the stories people tell themselves and others. Used deftly, point of view exposes the unjustified assumptions underlying supposed self-disclosure.

Such assumptions can cloud the judgment of either an individual or an entire group. That's the case on the first page of David Guterson's *Snow Falling on Cedars*. This is a novel about racism, whether thinly veiled or blatantly overt.

The townspeople of the fictitious San Piedro Island see the Japanese defendant, Kabuo Miyamoto, standing perfectly erect in the courtroom. Without questioning whether this posture is natural for him, the spectators immediately leap to hostile conclusions. To them, his stance clearly indicates fear, arrogance, guilt, or all of the above. They don't understand anything about him. Nor do they try.

Why would his stance necessarily signal pride or guilt rather than stoicism in the face of injustice? Does this community automatically condemn an innocent man, and if so, why? WWII is the answer, but Guterson *shows* rather than *tells* that. And the narrator begins subtly conveying this theme in the very first paragraph.

Used skillfully, point of view raises the questions that sharpen perception. How much fun can readers have if the novel answers everything it asks? *Faux clairvoyance* and unreliable narration intrigue to the same extent that point of view violations annoy. Differentiate inadvertent violations from deliberate techniques.

TIP
Watch what your narrator offers more carefully than your readers will.

Of course readers never want to notice the story's delivery. That's like a magician waving the scarves that hide the rabbit. The mystery vanishes, and with it, the most intriguing questions that fiction can pose: What do the characters seem to know? Why do they seem to know it? And what does this reveal about what readers think they know?

Questions about illusion versus truth pervade every genre. In romance, characters pursue genuine rather than superficial love, while in detective stories they chase the actual instead of apparent criminal. Thrillers portray protagonists seeking the right path amid all the enticing wrong ones. Nearly every novel follows someone searching for truth or resisting it.

That's because, like Oedipus Rex, most characters are blind to what they could or should see. Only at the climax does the protagonist discover what the narrator always knew. Plot gives deserving characters happiness. Point of view helps readers understand how and why that happened.

> **TIP**
> At its best, point of view investigates and unravels truth.

Point of View and Publishing

Understandably, writers gravitate toward the familiar, popular, or easy, especially when they see published novels treating point of view carelessly or inconsistently. Character thoughts sometimes appear in italics, sometimes not. Perspectives shift without transition or justification. If you notice this in bestsellers, it's easy to rationalize taking the easy way out yourself. Maybe when the tension's high, readers won't mind a little cheating. Besides, isn't everyone doing it?

Only you can choose between a quick fix and the ingenuity that challenge often summons. Just as *pressure points* stimulate the best in characters, point of view constraints stimulate the best in writers. Why rob yourself of potential inspiration? Or deprive readers of the consistency they deserve? Or jeopardize the ambiguity that makes novels credible and textured?

Of course taste and genre determine what a particular audience finds taxing or patronizing. Young adult readers usually prefer first person. Since point of view shifts complicate, roving and omniscient both seem more literary.

Aware of these realities, agents and publishers sometimes insist that all YA novels be first person, that omniscient is obsolete, or that first person outside of YA is self-indulgent. Consider these trends and prejudices, but don't let them completely sway you. Like point of view itself, the optimal perspective for your story and readers offsets potential difficulties with assets.

> **TIP**
> Why not consider point of view constraints to be creative opportunities?

✔ **Checklist Exercise**: Empowering Point of View

☐ Have you chosen the point of view best for this novel?

☐ Have you chosen the point of view best for its genre?

☐ Do you exploit your point of view's assets while minimizing its difficulties?

☐ Have you created a narrator readers want to follow?

☐ Does the narrator speculate enough but not too much?

☐ Do both characters and narrator contribute to every *scene*?

☐ Does your point of view invite reflection on the nature of truth?

↬**Exercise**: Polishing Your Chosen Point of View

Compare and contrast your writing strengths and weaknesses with those inherent in your point of view. If these clash impossibly, breathe deep and do what you must. However, as is likelier, revise to showcase strengths while downplaying weaknesses. You may find it helpful to revise thinking only about point of view, perhaps making notes on any other issues you notice during this particular read-through.

And so...

Readers want point of view to surprise them with its revelation of reality—not with its inconsistencies. Point of view belongs to the narrator, who determines suspense, pace, perception, even bookstore location. With so much at stake, you must manage the shortcomings of your chosen point of view, because, by definition, the stance of every narrator eliminates certain possibilities.

One of the author's tasks is to distribute storytelling responsibility between narrator and characters. You want to infer what readers probably want, using that presumption to choose between *scene* or *summary*, proximity or panorama, and emphasis on character emotion or behavior. Sound complicated? It is. To disappear from the story, an author must juggle many variables.

Happily, one system helps diagnose prose in terms of character or narrator prominence. It's called Character Presence, or CP, and the next chapter reveals how to apply it first for assessment, then revision.

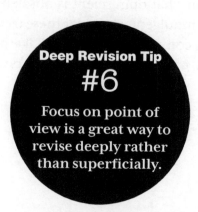

Deep Revision Tip
#6
Focus on point of view is a great way to revise deeply rather than superficially.

Delivery

Character + Narrator

Invaluable as instinct is, it won't necessarily put you in your readers' shoes. Do you know when the characters seem wooden—or if the timing's off? Readers do. They notice anything missing or overdone.

Along with that, readers sense whether they encounter characters directly or indirectly. One moment might feel like watching a film—with nothing separating the reader from the character. In contrast, the narrator's interpretation feels more remote.

Either directly from the character or indirectly through the narrator is one component of reader experience. Panorama or close-up is a second. Third, at this moment, do the details deliver internal thought and feeling, or external setting, behavior, and appearance?

To complete the fictional world, readers need it all: narrator interpretation and character interaction, breadth and immediacy, action and emotion. To assess the balance of these categories as the novel progresses, novelists need detachment. Yet it's difficult to evaluate your own writing: you've seen it too often, perhaps like it too well.

Fortunately, a strategy exists for cultivating objectivity. Character Presence (CP) diagnoses the magic underlying fiction, so you can do some enchanting of your own.

●◆ **Character Presence (CP):** A system classifying each sentence excluding dialogue as a) filtered through narrator or direct through character b) distant or close, and c) physical or intangible.

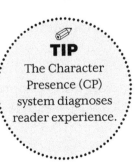

TIP
The Character Presence (CP) system diagnoses reader experience.

Just as many of the best novels help readers see the world a little differently, many of those novels originated with an author seeing the world a little differently. Change the way you perceive your manuscript, and you'll detect startling new possibilities. That's an essential benefit of Character Presence (CP): alter the perspective, and you can generate electric creativity.

Like a flashlight revealing what's right in front of you, Character Presence (CP) illuminates three variables that might otherwise escape detection:

- **Source**: Is this sentence the narrator framing the story, or the characters living it?

- **Distance**: Does this sentence reflect breadth or proximity?

- **Imagery**: Does this sentence present external behavior and description, or internal thought and feeling?

In every point of view, the interaction between source, distance, and imagery translates into five Character Presence levels.

TIP
Character Presence (CP) uses individual sentences to assess entire passages.

On Numbers and Novelists

Myth CP is useless unless each sentence indisputably represents one level.

The CP system uses numbers to classify sentences. Yet numbers can never precisely parallel subjective experience, whether that's pain, anger, or prose. Then why numbers? Though they can't make perception objective, they definitely make it less subjective. By assigning numbers, the CP system encourages impartiality, innovation, and flexibility. Because once you internalize the system, its numbers let you scan a passage and know if you've achieved the balance that you—and your readers!—want.

In any case, numbers are more elusive than they might seem; a continuum exists even between five and four. Writing issues are more slippery still; ten different writing coaches define *telling* ten slightly different ways. Numbers make some writers cringe, and others expect the consistency of 2 + 2 = 4. With no exceptions.

Yet with CP, exceptions do exist. Factors like point of view and tone influence how first writer, then reader perceive the presence of narrator or character. This ambiguity isn't important, because the numbers exist only to approximate the frequency and placement of the three CP variables across its five levels. Are these paragraphs too remote? Is this portrait incomplete? Do you use one component excessively? The purpose of CP is to notice whether you deliver what you intended.

TIP
CP diagnoses source, distance, and imagery—regardless of how casually or precisely you use its numbers.

Goldilocks and The Character Presence (CP) Levels

The CP System

CP diagnoses the thrust of each sentence:

- a) **Source:** Filtered through narrator—or direct from character.

- b) **Distance:** Panorama—or close up.

- c) **Tangibility:** External behavior and description—or internal thinking and feeling.

The Five CP Levels

- **Context (CP5):** The narrator level. Indirect. Filtered.

- **Insight (CP4):** The narrator interprets the character. Internal. Indirect. Filtered.

- **Shared (CP3):** Narrator and character, internal and external. Both direct and filtered.

- **Mindread (CP2):** Character internal. Direct. Unfiltered.

- **Zoom-in (CP1):** Character external. Direct. Unfiltered.

With CP, you can identify input from the narrator or character, and from what distance and tangibility.

CP in a Bedtime Story

Here's Goldilocks illustrating the five CP levels:

Third person:

Once upon a time an ursine family lived in a forest (**Context - CP5**). Not knowing this, a little girl wondered how it would feel to do some wandering (**Insight - CP4**). Certain she had nothing to fear, Goldilocks walked deep into the woods (**Shared - CP3**). Inviting little cabin to check out (**CP2 - Mindread**). In its kitchen, she was tasting the third bowl of porridge when the door creaked open (**Zoom-in - CP1**).

First person:

> Once upon a time an ursine family lived in a forest (**Context - CP5**). Not knowing this, I wondered how it would feel to do some wandering (**Insight - CP4**). With nothing to fear, I walked deep into the woods (**Shared - CP3**). Inviting little cabin to check out (**CP2 - Mindread**). In its kitchen, I was tasting the third bowl of porridge when the door creaked open (**Zoom-in - CP1**).

As the mini-version above descends through the five CP levels, the narrator eventually disappears, drawing readers closer to the main character. Notice that with Context (CP5) and Mindread (CP2), certain sentences don't change when the point of view does.

What else? Because the passage above is only for illustration, the CP levels proceed downward from one level to the next. Under normal circumstances, though, no novelist would ever intentionally descend or ascend through the CP levels!

Instead, CP lets you assess so you can adjust. Don't try using it to impose a particular order, distribute the levels in equal amounts, or any other rigid pattern.

Ready for more specifics? The tale about too much, too little, or just right can offer a more detailed illustration of how the five CP levels operate:

> **TIP**
> The purpose of Character Presence (CP) is diagnosis, never any sort of formula.

● Context (CP5, or narrator only)

Distant. Narrator view. Setting or generality without individuals. Filtered.

Example: Big trees surrounded a little house.

Example: Little girls should watch where they wander.

In first or third person point of view, the narrator's delivery of CONTEXT often sounds identical. This level provides setting, information, or observation. From this distance, a crowd might be visible, but no individual is distinct.

Next? CP4 (Insight) introduces character, but only internally and via the narrator.

Contrast:

CP5 - Context: Clouds darkened the landscape.

with

CP4 - Insight: Her/my thoughts swung between excited and scared.

● Insight (CP4, or internal character via narrator)

Less distant. Narrator analyzing character feelings. Inner view. Filtered.

Third Person example: Goldilocks felt worried and terribly alone.

First Person example: I never felt this worried or lost.

The narrator supplies INSIGHT into the internal world of character thought and feeling. No literal physical description.

Next? CP3 (Shared) integrates narrator with character to portray a character completely—inside and out.

Contrast:

CP4 - Insight: Goldilocks started being adventurous at an early age.

with

CP3 - Shared: Though she'd never seen these trees before, Goldilocks bent to tighten her shoelaces and decided to go just a little farther.

● Shared (CP3, or external and internal narrator and character)

Midway. Full view: narrator + character, internal + external. Filtered and direct.

Third Person example: Goldilocks shivered, wanting someplace to hide.

First Person example: The noise made me shiver and hope for a place to hide.

Narrator and character SHARE presentation of character emotion and conduct. CP3 (Shared) covers all the CP variables.

Next? In CP2 (Mindread), the narrator disappears, drawing readers closer to the character.

Contrast:

> **CP3 - Shared:** Picking up a spoon to taste the porridge, Goldilocks hoped no one was home.

with

> **CP2 - Mindread:** Smells great, but sure hope no one's around.

● Mindread (CP2, or internal character)

Close. Internal view of character without narrator input. Direct, internal, unfiltered.

Third Person example: Oh, oh, time for her to get the heck out. But how?

First Person example: Oh, oh, time for me to get the heck out. But how?

Readers get to MINDREAD intimate character thoughts and feelings. By eliminating the narrator, CP2 (Mindread) offers a direct inner character view.

Next? CP1 (Zoom-in) photographs the external character.

Contrast:

> **CP2 - Mindread:** Was someone out there?

with

> **CP1 - Zoom-in:** Crawling under the table, Goldilocks stubbed her toe.

TIP

CP helps you choose between too much, too little, or just the right amounts of character, distance, and physicality.

● Zoom-in (CP1, or external character)

Closest. External character without narrator. Direct, external, unfiltered.

Third Person example: She crouched beneath the kitchen table.

First Person example: I crouched beneath the kitchen table.

Readers ZOOM in on external details about character behavior or appearance. No internal, analysis, or narrator commentary.

CP in Action

Whether children's story or novel, CP works the same. Here's another illustration:

Third person:

> Few women admired their own modernity and chutzpah more than Emmeline (Insight - CP4). Any savvy woman, faced with a Goldilocks predicament, can deftly maneuver between too much or little responsibility and land the perfect career (Context - CP5). Convinced of this, Emmeline ignored the doorman whose gaze raked her slightly outdated skirt (Shared - CP3). Way too grand a company (Mindread - CP2). She straightened her shoulders, and nose aimed at the glass ceiling, fled a start-up techie in a leaky, Salvation-army-furnished loft (Shared - CP3). Too small (Mindread - CP2). Seventeen dead-end interviews altered her perspective (Insight - CP4). Are you still a firebrand if your hair's red because you dye it (Mindread - CP2)? Shoulders slumped, she entered a one-story building (Zoom-in - CP1). Goldilocks was for kids (Mindread - CP2).

First person:

> I've long admired modernity and chutzpah (Insight - CP4). Any savvy woman, faced with a Goldilocks predicament, can deftly maneuver between too much or little responsibility to land the perfect career (Context - CP5). Certain of this, I ignored the doorman whose gaze raked my slightly outdated skirt (Shared - CP3). Way too grand a company (Mindread - CP2). I straightened my shoulders, aimed my nose at the glass ceiling, and fled a start-up techie in a leaky, Salvation-army-furnished loft (Shared - CP3). Too small (Mindread - CP2). Seventeen dead-end interviews changed my perspective (Insight - CP4). Am I still a firebrand if my hair's red because I dye it (Mindread - CP2)? Shoulders slumped, I entered a one-story building (Zoom-in - CP1). Goldilocks was for kids (Mindread - CP2).

Both the third person and first person versions cover all five CP possibilities (source, physicality, and distance). But few paragraphs have or need every Character Presence level. Nor, as the example above demonstrates, is the purpose of CP delivering the levels either in fixed amounts or laboriously arranging them in ascending, descending, or any particular order.

Instead, use CP to constantly evaluate reader needs within a particular section. Narrator or character? Physical or internal? Distant or close? You can see what you have so you can see whether you want what you have.

Choosing the CP Level You Need

This overview helps you provide the completeness readers deserve.

- Comprehensive:

    Shared (CP3)

- Tangible:

    Context (CP5 originating from narrator)

    Zoom-in (CP1 exhibited by character)

- Emotional or introspective:

    Insight (CP4 originating from narrator)

    Mindread (CP2 exhibited by character)

- Immediate:

    Mindread (CP2 internal character)

    Zoom-in (CP1 external character)

- Broad, geographical, historical:

    Context (CP5 originating from narrator)

TIP
Character Presence (CP) helps you read like a reader.

CP and Revision

If you go no further than simply keeping in mind the three CP variables (source, distance, physicality), you'll still have both new awareness along with alternative solutions to whatever imbalance you detect. Might this sentence move closer to the character? Further away? Such possibilities open the new pathways that are key to creative revision.

Perhaps you've had the experience of vowing to rework a section until it succeeds, only to produce one listless version after another. Frustration rarely yields ingenuity. Neither does clinging to one approach when so many other possibilities are just beyond reach. Want inspiration? Alter the view.

CP undercuts the natural desire to justify what's written, stimulating you to add or subtract as needed. Does the narrator dominate? Would breadth escalate tension, or do you need more intimacy? CP reminds you to assess what your story needs. Is anything overdone or missing?

✔ **Checklist Exercise:** Changing the CP Level

You can shake things up with questions like these:

☐ Do you overuse narrator, internal, close, or their opposites?

☐ Does every *scene* offer the full range of CP variables?

☐ Do you exploit the capacity of fiction to offer both the external world of environment and behavior plus the character's inner world?

☐ Does the narrator filter *scenes* while the characters invigorate *summary*?

☐ Have you tried delivering a troublesome sentence at a different CP level?

TIP

The CP (Character Presence) system solves common writing problems with the diagnosis that facilitates deep revision.

Character Presence (CP) Overview

Who, What, Where	Purposes
Context: CP5 - furthest from character Either tangible or abstract narrator overview No individual character visible	Establish the novel's world Depict environment Ground with setting, fact, history, theory
Insight: CP4 - closer to character Narrator interpretation of character mind No physical detail	Analyze character motive and response Dispense psychology and backstory Explain what the character can't or won't
Shared: CP3 - still closer to character Narrator + character for full picture Behavior, appearance, emotions, thoughts	Synthesize the benefits of film and fiction Provide comprehensive characterization Integrate external and internal character
Mindread: CP2 - close to character Uncensored internal responses No narrator or physical detail	Penetrate character psyche Convey gut reactions Add clairvoyance, intimacy, irony
Zoom-in CP1 - closest to character Character behavior and appearance No narrator or character thought	Create the illusion of film Show how characters act and look Encourage reader inference

Context (CP5)—the setting or society-shaping characters.

> **Example:** Sunset can seem symbolic.

Insight (CP4)—narrator interpreting character emotion.

> **Example:** Memories of sunset scared him/me.

Shared (CP3)—all-inclusive character.

> **Example:** She/I smiled, recalling past sunsets.

Mindread (CP2)—uncensored character response.

> **Example:** Just a blasted sunset.

Zoom-in (CP1)—character conduct or appearance.

> **Example:** He/I raced toward the setting sun.

Comparison/Contrast of the CP
(Character Presence) Levels

CP5 (Context): Setting and overview from narrator. Indirect and filtered.

Examples:

Only human emotion invests the full moon with enmity or sainthood.

In the thin sunlight the ice-enshrouded red twig dogwoods cast gnarled shadows.

Like most everything organic, humans are phototropic.

CP5 (Context) Cautions

· Compensate for lack of conflict with originality, humor, lyricism, etc.

· Avoid abstraction.

· Know your audience, key to the amount and kind of information readers seek.

· Resist educating, however great the temptation.

CP5 (Context) Opportunities

● **Foreshadowing**.

Background can intensify drama. Frederick Forsyth's *The Day of the Jackal* opens with time, location, weather and—an imminent execution.

● **Setting**.

Combine several of the five senses to describe landscape. Joan Slonczewski creates the underwater world of *A Door into Ocean* using not only exotic sights, but smells and sounds to accompany them.

● **Atmosphere**.

The physical climate can mirror and help capture the emotional one. Not just it's "hot," but "The heat seemed to drain everyone present of their individuality, their humanity."

CP4 (Insight): Access to character emotion and backstory through narrator. Indirect and filtered.

Examples:

I pride myself on my paucity of virtue.

Mark's devotion to opera was more survival instinct than predilection.

Francine was so accustomed to Bob mistreating her that any other behavior felt treacherous.

CP4 (Insight) Cautions

- Maintain tension by avoiding *emotional shorthand,* such as fury or ecstacy.
- Reserve CP4 (Insight) for details readers can't infer, such as the suicide of the antagonist's father or the reason your protagonist never complains.
- Reduce abstraction with non-clichéd imagery, e.g., "Ann's mom dreaded falling the way Columbus dreaded plummeting off the edge of the earth."

CP4 (Insight) Opportunities

● **Compassion.**

Only the narrator can explain the motivation, insight, or backstory that promotes full empathy:

She'd waitressed ten hours a day to put him through law school and now he figured he'd trade up for a newer model.

● **Dimension.**

Narrators possess insight that characters lack.

Like Matt Damon in "Good Will Hunting," neither townie nor preppy, Robbie was a kid without a country.

● **Irony.**

CP4 (Insight) can accentuate how rarely we receive what we want or expect:

Two days after he agreed to marry me, Jackson crept out in the middle of the night to buy cigarettes and never returned.

● **Transition**.

CP4 (Insight) can shift time by tracking the changing emotional atmosphere.

As the weeks disappeared, he became increasingly alarmed at the prospect of this tiny stranger who'd destroy the life they'd built.

CP3 (Shared): Character + narrator reveal external and internal character. Both direct and filtered.

Examples:

The sight of the massacred doll, its plastic head dangling from the shattered neck, reminded Martina of her dad smacking all of them around.

Rain thrummed on the tin roof, evoking memories of Gram holding me as we listened together.

Thomasina hadn't called ahead, so Michael cracked his knuckles, one by one, trying to decide if he should meet her at the airport or stay put.

CP3 (Shared) Cautions

- Avoid *single-pronged emotions* so the internal component doesn't *tell*.
- Provide the passion of characters going at it in a live *scene* (CP1- Zoom-in) rather than making love—or anything else—over a span of days (CP3 - Shared).
- Select concrete and specific wording. Not "Mike headed home perplexed about honesty," but "As Mike trudged past the houses without yards, he debated keeping the wallet."

CP3 (Shared) Opportunities

● **Synthesis**.

Readers simultaneously experience action and reaction.

The astonished betrayal in the dog's eyes signaled that this was no way to train anyone.

● **Imagery**.

Physicality substantiates emotion:

CP3 Shared imparts physicality to the abstractness of emotion. For example, Bernard Malamud introduces us to the protagonist of *The Natural* with the vibrant image of Roy Hobbs lighting a match and finding his own face reflected back at him in the train window.

● **Transition**.

Concrete details can advance time. In old movies, flipping calendar pages did it. Now you'll need something more like "As I always did when waiting, I chewed each remnant of fingernail, methodically progressing until I'd completed all ten."

● **Faux Clairvoyance**.

The narrator can use observation and experience to speculate:

When Alyssa's voice trembled as she answered, Samuel knew she'd detected his lie.

CP2 (Mindread):Intimate access to character emotion. Internal, direct, and unfiltered.

Examples:

Never again. Not in this lifetime. Or any other.

Oh sure, how about forgiveness all around.

A miniature snapshot of heaven on earth.

CP2 (Mindread) Cautions

· Omit the *telling* CP2 (Mindread) can include.

· Capture thought credibly with an informal tone.

· Maintain pronoun and verb tense consistency.

CP2 (Mindread) Opportunities

● **Confession**.

Readers relish inadvertent self-disclosure: "If I could I'd wipe out every one of those scumbags."

- **Foreshadowing.**

Hint the future and emphasize significance: "What a piece of evidence. What a sloppy criminal. What amazing good fortune."

- **Irony.**

Give readers the pleasure of seeing what the character didn't: "Fairest of them all. Who could compete?"

CP1 (Zoom-in): character behavior or description. External, direct, and unfiltered.

Examples:

Clark dialed Lois's number.

Alain leapt across the stage to his counterpart, inhaled, and lifted the ballerina above his shoulders.

I kept my lips clamped shut as the tiger limped toward me.

CP1 (Zoom-in) Cautions

- · Offer some filmable moments that are neither judgmental nor ongoing.

- · Choose specific, concrete verbs, i.e. "strolled" or "yawned" instead of "moved" or "turned."

- · Eliminate cliché, especially about tears or smiles.

CP1 (Zoom-in) Opportunities

- **Cinema.**

Direct access to the character in the physical world: "The skater completed his Quad only nine inches away from the judges leaning over the desk."

- **Speaker attribution.**

CP1 (Zoom-in) grounds dialogue and indicates who's talking: "Penelope giggled. 'Why wouldn't you'?"

● **Tension.**

Give high-stakes moments the immediacy they deserve: "I pulled my knife. Dan shook his head and squinted his eyes as I pointed it between us."

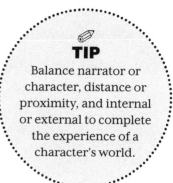

TIP

Balance narrator or character, distance or proximity, and internal or external to complete the experience of a character's world.

And so...

The violin produces many agonizing squeaks before it offers music. In contrast, the instrument of CP rewards instantly, because it heightens sensitivity to the choice and position of details. Change your perception of delivery, intimacy, and tangibility, and the quality of your perception changes. This affects your ability to revise deeply and creatively. Immediately.

Of course, like practicing an instrument, CP produces the best results for those most skilled with it. Master the fundamentals, and you can advance to nuance. How can CP assist with point of view limitations? Or reveal what a character doesn't know? Or identify writing habits you want to break? The next chapter applies CP to the issues that every novelist faces.

Deep Revision Tip

#7

Readers expect novels to surprise them.

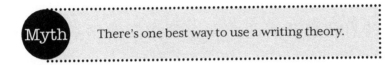

Character Presence (CP)

Vision and Revision

Myth   There's one best way to use a writing theory.

Not at all. For instance, in *The Writer's Journey*, Christopher Vogler briefly summarizes the twelve stages that a protagonist experiences, then offers a detailed snapshot of each. This approach accommodates different learning styles. Will you find a theory most valuable if you have lots of specifics, or would you prefer a general overview? Or, would you like to switch back and forth between the two?

This book offers similar options. Want a thorough and detailed examination of CP? Supplement the material in this chapter with the even more complete portrait of each level in the appendix. Eager to start applying CP for revision without additional analysis? You'll find the basics in this chapter. And, if that's still too much detail, just revise using the general characteristics of each level that the preceding chapter covered.

All of these approaches work. Personal inclination determines whether you want to know a little less or a little more. Only you understand how much detail will promote the most effective diagnosis and revision of your novel. Whatever you decide, you can still use CP (Character Presence) to assess the distribution of filtered or direct, external or internal, and remote or more intimate.

TIP

CP (Character presence) lets you grasp the big picture.

How to Get the Most from CP (Character Presence)

These questions, gathered from writers familiar with CP, clarify the system so you can implement it more efficiently and successfully. First, a more detailed look at each level.

● **What are the characteristics of CP5 (Context)?**

Narrator only. Physical or non-physical. Filtered.

The worldview level offers only the narrator, whether providing setting or observations. Since the narrator describes the broad picture without differentiated individuals, this level is indirect and furthest from the characters.

CP5 grounds readers by supplying **context**, which encompasses setting, theory, or fact. Because CP5 (Context) is the narrator's province, it tends to sound distant and omniscient. Its tone encompasses biased or impartial, abstract or concrete, and literal or symbolic.

Snapshot of CP5 (Context)—story world filtered through narrator.

Example: The moon illuminated the mountain peaks, leaving the army in shadow.

Example: Both bees and beekeepers know the secrets of honey.

Presence: Narrator. No differentiated character in view.

Distance from character: Furthest. Impossible to distinguish individuals from this range.

Tangibility: Everything from physical setting to abstract concept.

Goal: To anchor—landscape, philosophy, information.

● **What distinguishes CP5 (Context) from comparable levels?**

Here's how three different CP levels present similar observations:

CP5 (Context)	CP4 (Insight)	CP2 (Mindread)
Most distant	Distant	Close
Sociological	Psychological	Personal
Theoretical truth	Truth about a character	Character version of truth
Narrator only	Character via narrator	Character only
"Few love history."	"Eli/I hated history."	"History—pile of dung."

● **What are the assets and possible disadvantages of CP5 (Context)?**

CP5 (Context) Contributions	CP5 (Context) Possible Drawbacks
Setting	Cliché
Atmosphere	Plot interruption
Grounding	Excessive information or abstraction
Framework	*Telling*

TIP
At its best,
CP5 (Context)
heightens conflict
by interpreting
the character's
world.

☞**Exercise**: Hooking with CP5 (Context)

Revise several *scene* openings in your novel by infusing setting with tension, e.g. not "The rain continued," but "Rain flooded the pass, blocking access to food and medical supplies."

● **What are the characteristics of CP4 (Insight)?**

Narrator about inner character. Non-physical. Filtered.

The narrator analyzes character thoughts and emotions. This level is less indirect, because the internal character is revealed, but only through the narrator. Readers still feel distant from the characters.

CP4 provides **insight**, because the narrator illuminates motivation that the characters neither completely understand nor willingly divulge. Readers gain access to the multi-faceted emotions of the characters.

●◆ **Multi-Faceted Emotion**: A dynamic, complex, and thus realistic expression of a feeling, such as lust tinged with guilt, fear, pity, or a mixture of those.

Readers crave the realism of layered rather than single-pronged emotions.

●◆ **Single-Pronged Emotion**: An oversimplified reduction of a many-layered response like envy into superficial, abstract, unrealistic *emotional shorthand*.

Snapshot of CP4 (Insight)—character psychology through narrator.

Example: Thanksgiving represented everything the dowager despised.

Example: My wife's interminable euphemisms disturbed me on a daily basis.

Presence: Narrator. Indirect analysis of inner character. Filtered.

Distance from character: Still far. Internal character available only through narrator.

Tangibility: Abstract except for symbolic description.

Goal: To probe—revelation of character reaction, background, and choices.

● **What distinguishes CP4 (Insight) from comparable levels?**

Here's the distinction between the narrator describing emotion and the character experiencing it:

CP4 (Insight)	CP2 (Mindread)
Narrator and character	Character only
Addresses reader	Addresses self
Knows what's ahead	No idea what's ahead
Interprets	Reacts
Contemplative	Colloquial
Theme-oriented	Plot-oriented
"Ed/I valued achievement, not integrity."	"Busted. Again."

● **What are the assets and possible disadvantages of CP4 (Insight)?**

CP4 (Insight) Contributions	CP4 (Insight) Possible Drawbacks
Summary	*Telling*
Rationale	*Telling*
Motive	*Telling*
Irony	Cliché
Backstory	Abstraction

⌒▸**Exercise**: Reducing Abstraction

Add a symbolic comparison to an abstract emotional analysis in your novel, such as, "Loneliness made him feel like a starving dog poking through other people's trash."

● **What are the characteristics of CP3 (Shared)?**

Narrator and character. Physical and non-physical. Still partially filtered.

This level incorporates the entire compendium of everything outside dialogue. At mid-distance between remote narrator and accessible character, CP3 (Shared) combines narrator with character and external with internal.

CP3 occurs frequently in fiction, because narrator and character **share** the stage, combining behavior with emotion. This makes CP3 a wonderful source of comprehensiveness and. transition

Snapshot of CP3 (Shared)—physical and emotional through character and narrator.

Example: Though Ed cherished wildness, he corralled the stallion as instructed.

Example: My mirror reflected eyes that no longer believed in dreams coming true.

Presence: Narrator and character both. All-inclusive view of character. Still filtered.

Distance from character: Intermediate. Narrator still present.

Tangibility: Multi-dimensional.

Goal: To fuse—integration of external and internal character.

● **What are the assets and possible disadvantages of CP3 (Context)?**

CP3 (Shared) Contributions	CP3 (Shared) Possible Drawbacks
Hook	*Telling*
Transition	Overuse of *collapsed time*
Stage business	Unnecessary narrator input

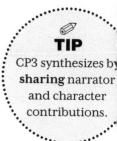
TIP
CP3 synthesizes by **sharing** narrator and character contributions.

↪**Exercise**: Integrating Inner and Outer Views

Add a physical component in order to change at least five CP4 (Insight) sentences from your novel to CP3 (Shared).

● **What are the characteristics of CP2 (Mindread)?**

Character only. Non-physical. Unfiltered.

At this level, nothing separates the reader from one character's thoughts and feelings. Without the narrator, readers directly access the character's inner world, making this is a close, intimate level.

CP2 lets readers **mindread**, satisfying our curiosity about the thoughts few people willingly reveal.

Snapshot of CP2 (Mindread)—unfiltered access to uninhibited character emotion.

Example: Nauseating. The unrivaled luxury of draping yourself in dead animal pelts.

Example: Diamonds. Still a girl's best friend.

Presence: Character. Direct and internal. No narrator. Unfiltered.

Distance from character: Close.

Tangibility: None.

Goal: To eavesdrop—unimpeded access to the character's most private self.

● **What distinguishes CP2 (Mindread) from comparable levels?**

Particularly in first person, only the tone and surrounding sentences distinguish character feelings from narrator observations.

Here's the breakdown:

CP5 (Context)	CP4 (Insight)	CP2 (Mindread)
Narrator only	Narrator + character	Character only
Formal	Formal	Uncensored
Philosophical	Psychoanalytical	Personal
Universal	Specific	Private
Theme-oriented	Plot-oriented	Plot-oriented
"Light compels."	"Light lets her/me bloom."	"Never enough light."

● **What are the assets and possible disadvantages of CP2 (Mindread)?**

CP2 (Mindread) Contributions	CP2 (Mindread) Possible Drawbacks
Intimacy	Tense bumps
Empathy	Pronoun bumps
Wit	Cuteness
Dramatic irony	*Telling*
Passion	Communicating the obvious

↬**Exercise**: Sharpening dialogue

Select some dialogue from your novel where you could add snarky CP2 (Mindread), as in "How about I help you lift that," she suggested. Unless you enjoy calling 911.

TIP

CP2 fosters intimacy via **mindread**.

● **What are the characteristics of CP1 (Zoom-in)?**

Character only. Physical. Completely unfiltered.

No narrator and nothing internal. This unobstructed view of behavior and appearance brings readers closest to the characters.

Whether *real time* or flashback, CP1 lets readers directly **zoom in** on character behavior, gesture, and appearance. Characters waltz, throw snowballs, load guns, wear fur boots. In CP1 (Zoom-in), nothing separates the audience from the exterior character, so George Orwell might have called this the "windowpane" level.

Snapshot of CP1 (Zoom-in)—character behavior and appearance without narrator filter.

Example: Clark dialed Lois's number.

Example: Maintaining eye contact with the HR guy, I extended my right hand.

Presence: Character. External. No narrator.

Distance from character: Close. Nothing isolates reader from character conduct or appearance.

Tangibility: Total.

Goal: To film—movie sequence of character interaction.

● **What distinguishes CP1 from comparable levels?**

CP5 (Context)	CP3 (Shared)	CP1 (Zoom-in)
No distinct character	Narrator and character	Character without narrator
General environment	Complete character portrait	Physical character only
Customers surged inside.	Ted/I warily shrank back.	Ted/I limped into the store.
Yellow is a beloved color.	Ann/I flaunted a yellow bra.	Ann/I wore a yellow bra.

● **What are the assets and possible disadvantages of CP1 (Zoom - in)?**

CP1 (Zoom-in) Contributions	CP1 (Zoom-in) Possible Drawbacks
Accessibility	Cliché
Tension	No internal view
Immediacy	No narrator insight
Momentum	Harried pace

✑**Exercise**: Enriching Stage Business

Replace over-used gestures in your book like shrugging or balling into fists with original imagery like:

> Herman spoke through a mouthful of onion rings (CP1 - Zoom-in.) "I deserve a treat (Dialogue)."
>
> Hortense glared at his paunch (CP1 - Zoom-in). "Does your cholesterol count deserve one, too (Dialogue)?"

TIP

CP1 **zooms in** to deliver the immediacy of film.

● **Why doesn't every sentence unequivocally represent one CP level or another?**

Because words are ambiguous. Take "slouched." If it's considered neutral, then "She slouched" is CP1 (Zoom-in). But if "slouched" signals narrator interpretation of a physical action, then the sentence is CP3 (Shared).

This isn't a significant discrepancy because—CP's purpose isn't assigning numbers! Whether with individual sentences or entire pages, the CP system helps you imagine how a reader might experience your novel. You needn't squander a single precious writing moment fussing about numbers: you're only trying to swiftly assess which of the three CP variables (source, distance, physicality) you perhaps overdid or underutilized.

However, you can use those numbers to improve detachment, insight, and creativity. Keep CP in mind and, eventually, you'll evaluate its components almost automatically. Many writers find that the numbers speed the internalization process.

● **Why do readers need external and internal, distance and proximity?**

To make fiction seem real and complete. In order to maximize drama and empathy, think about source, distance, and physicality as you select which details to include. For example, in *The Boleyn Inheritance* by Philippa Gregory, readers don't hear about pain, banishment, or remorse. Such words accomplish little.

Abstract language is the conventional treatment for describing crushed fantasies. But what can that tired, familiar language evoke? Will it make readers feel what the characters do?

Instead, in eighty-five words Gregory portrays everything from the mud beneath the protagonist's fingertips to the road that connects with London, which stretches out of sight.

A comprehensive merger of external and internal, close and distant, lets readers vicariously experience the protagonist's plight. And avoids the likelihood of cliché.

Why wouldn't writers automatically offer readers this kind of comprehensive portrait? Probably because writers associate emotion with CP4 (Insight) and action with CP1 (Zoom-in). But custom can undermine opportunity. Raise the stakes by adding physicality to emotion and revelation to action. Exploit surprise. You might be surprised by how well this works.

TIP

Fiction must both meet and defy expectations.

● How can CP intensify emotion and suspense?

By gauging timing. Like jokes, fiction soars or flops based on the precision and progression of details. Towards the end of *The Amazing Adventures of Kavalier and Klay*, Michael Chabon must capture a mother's preparations for the reunion that their clever son engineered for his parents. This woman experiences the gamut of emotions: love for her child, gratitude over seeing her husband after all this time, fear that he'll find her changed, and anxiety over how to dress and what to say.

Too often, writers hope to portray distress by describing emotions alone. Why not capture anxiety with CP3 (Shared) and CP1 (Zoom-in), instead of only CP4 (Insight) and CP2 (Mindread)? Chabon reveals his character's state of mind with the nervous smearing of her lipstick and choice of macaroni and cheese. This is the way to go: blend *telling* about character feelings with *showing* them.

By offering a range of the CP levels within each scene, you can intensify conflict along with emotion. Perhaps one level recurs too often or at the wrong moment. Experimentation with CP can enhance every kind of tension, including *pressure points*.

A major one occurs in Alice Hoffman's *Here on Earth* when the antagonist, teenaged Hollis, is beaten and left bleeding in the snow. Readers enter a fully fleshed-out *scene*. A snowmobile whirrs in the background. Crows swoop through thick clouds.

Hoffman's details capture every aspect of the violence—from up close and at a distance, both in the internal world and the external one. Along with the characters, the reader inhabits this foreboding landscape. Readers can almost feel the blows, and that's partly because mechanical noise and grim weather are part of the *scene*.

But Hoffman doesn't dump a bunch of CP5 (Context) sentences in a row. Rather, she distributes them one at a time, supplementing rather than distracting from the thrashing and the responses of various characters to it.

Too often, writers reduce confrontation to a narrow focus: "The beating left him bleeding" (CP1 - Zoom-in) followed by "He knew then that he would never forgive them" (CP4 - Insight), and "How he hated them" (CP2 - Mindread).

Ideally, however, emotion is conveyed from all the angles available to a novelist. Avoid relying exclusively on the physical details of an attack (CP1 - Zoom-in) or the internal world (CP2 -Mindread and CP4 - Insight).

Clichés receive that label because they once haunted so much that everyone used them all the time. Now, though, they merely call attention to themselves. Instead of hoping that readers might not notice trite expressions, try something different. Portray trauma, or any intense emotion, with kaleidoscopic, innovative description that completes the portrait rather than offering only a limited, exhausted view.

Memorable *scenes* originate from details that both contribute on their own and work in unison as well. Like Hoffman, John Updike incorporates a variety of CP levels in a memorable *scene* from *Terrorist*.

An assassin awaits his accomplice. And readers wait right along with him. The view that Updike captures is all-encompassing. Today this street is quieter than usual (CP5 - Context). Ahmad doesn't just worry (CP4 - Insight and CP2 - Mindread). He checks his watch and looks around again (CP3 - Shared). Still alone now, he begins to panic (CP2 - Mindread). And when he concludes that God has abandoned him, the terrified realization strikes both externally and internally (CP3 - Shared). Updike succeeds in generating empathy for a potential terrorist.

> **TIP**
> No CP level is inherently superior, but one choice is often preferable at a given moment.

Why not select a few passages that you find particularly comprehensive, compelling, or crisp and analyze the CP levels? That's likely to generate ideas about how you can put CP to use in your own novel.

● **Are CP and point of view interconnected?**

Of course. Each system assesses the reader's experience of the character/narrator relationship. But point of view and CP approach this relationship from slightly different angles for very different purposes. Narrator breadth determines point of view, whether expansive omniscient, restricted third limited, or even more restricted first person.

> **TIP**
> CP helps you get the most from whichever point of view you choose.

In contrast, CP diagnoses reader experience: narrator or character, distance, and physicality. Obviously, point of view and CP also differ in range, respectively applying to either the entire novel or the individual sentence.

● **How does CP help the novelist revise point of view?**

By inviting questions about perception. How distant do the characters seem? Does delivery through the narrator or character encourage reader inference? Does the combination of external and internal details perfect the picture? CP assists by identifying character and narrator contributions from moment to moment.

> **TIP**
> CP reminds you to supply what's missing.

- **How can CP specifically assist with first-person narration?**

  Increasing awareness of "self-talk."

  ●◆ **Self-Talk:** the first-person narrator reproducing character thoughts that could be self-evident from behavior and dialogue.

  Of course every story needs the concreteness that CP1 (Zoom-in) and CP5 (Context) provide: executed powerfully, these levels let readers forget that they're reading.

  This first-person illustration emphasizes the world beyond the narrator's mind.

  > Silence (CP2 - Mindread). Too much of it (CP2 - Mindread). Trying not to think about emptiness or death, I opened the front door (CP3 - Shared). Then I let it squeal shut behind me (CP1 - Zoom-in). In the living room, each framed photograph tilted toward the lower side of the house (CP5 - Context). Dust covered everything (CP5 - Context). Cobwebs decorated the walls, and mouse droppings hid most of the carpet (CP5 - Context). I climbed the stairs (CP1 - Zoom-in). Breathing felt impossible (CP3 - Shared). Up there, the silence was worst of all (CP3 - Shared). Loud enough to remind of the voices you'd never hear again (CP2 - Mindread).

  Perhaps more than any other perspective, first person requires the grounding of the external levels: CP5 (Context), CP3 (Shared), and CP1 (Zoom-in). Tangibility offsets the intrusion of "I felt this" and "I wondered that." To break that habit, ask yourself what the setting looks like. What are the characters doing? Can you *show* what's going on instead of always *telling* about it? CP identifies whether you balance internal commentary detail with external description.

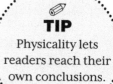

TIP
Physicality lets readers reach their own conclusions.

- **How can CP specifically assist with third-person limited narration?**

  By diagnosing internal and external balance. Here's an illustration:

  > Silence (CP2 - Mindread). Too much of it (CP2 - Mindread). Trying not to think about emptiness or death, Caitlin opened the front door (CP3 - Shared). Then she let it squeal shut behind her (CP1 - Zoom-in). In the living room, each framed photograph tilted toward the lower side of the house (CP5 - Context). Dust covered everything (CP5 - Context). Cobwebs decorated the walls, and mouse droppings hid most of the

carpet (CP5 - Context). She climbed the stairs (CP1 - Zoom-in). Breathing felt impossible (CP3 - Shared). Up there, the silence was worst of all (CP3 - Shared). Loud enough to remind of the voices she'd never hear again (CP2 - Mindread).

Much like first person, third limited benefits from the concreteness of CP5 (Context), CP3 (Shared), and CP1 (Zoom-in).

To gain further insight into the interaction between CP and point of view, scrutinize the three slightly different versions of this same passage. Look particularly at the sentence concluding the two passages above and the one below. What happens when the pronouns change? Identical or similar sentences sometimes feel like another level. Occasionally, too, an altered point of view might suggest that another CP level would be preferable.

TIP

Give readers all the CP variables, including those your point of view tends to minimize.

- **How can CP specifically assist with omniscient narration?**

By reminding to foster intimacy.

Silence (CP5 - Context). Too much of it (CP2 - Mindread). Where was the escape (CP2 - Mindread)? Trying not to think about emptiness or death, Oscar opened the front door (CP3 - Shared). Then he let it squeal shut behind him (CP1 - Zoom-in). In the living room, every framed photograph tilted toward the lower side of the house (CP5 - Context). Cobwebs decorated the walls, and mouse droppings hid most of the carpet (CP5 - Context). He climbed the stairs (CP1 - Zoom-in). Breathing felt impossible (CP3 - Shared). Up there, the silence was worst of all (CP3 - Shared). Like a grave (CP2 - Mindread). And loud enough to remind of the voices that'd never be heard again (CP5 - Context).

While this passage contains no facts regarding the physiology of silence or anecdotes detailing customs about death, it could. Omniscient perspective tends toward that direction, providing an opportunity for novelists who want to convey information.

But always offset CP5 (Context) with the other four levels. Include as much information as you wish—so long as it strengthens plot and characterization rather than overshadowing or competing with them. Readers who lose sight of the characters usually lose interest in the fiction. CP is a helpful reminder to balance the choice and placement of details.

TIP

Offer readers intimacy along with panorama.

● **How can I know how much CP5 (Context) is too much?**

Not surprisingly, it's hard to know, since many variables affect reader response. Some people read fiction to learn about Athens, woodworking, or another interest. And adroit use of setting adds credibility, richness, and deep characterization.

Still, as the most remote level, CP5 (Context) must reveal how the physical or intellectual climate shapes the characters. In contrast with CP levels 1 - 4, the most frequent use of CP5 (Context) is to support some other level.

So you need to use CP5 (Context) sparingly, and plan to infuse it with concrete details and perhaps poetic wording. The effectiveness of CP5 (Context) depends not only on language but what you describe. In other words, if the setting is exotic or you can render it so, then you can be more detailed. Otherwise? Tighten up.

Whenever the backdrop overwhelms character and plot, CP5 (Context) disappoints. Every protagonist inhabits a world that exerts pressure and promotes change. Use the setting and information that CP5 (Context) provide to elicit reader emotion.

TIP

The purpose of CP5 (Context) is not just world-building, but characterization.

● **How can CP improve individual paragraphs?**

With diagnosis. Readers need close and distant, expansive and restricted, character and narrator. Unless you offer all that, and time it successfully, you produce a blur like this first-person opening:

> Lake Superior's waves rolled in (CP5 - Context). It was cloudy (CP5 - Context). Hardly anyone was on the beach (CP5 - Context). My parents always insist that I watch my little brother (CP4 - Insight). What a drag (CP2 - Mindread). Such a jerk (CP2 - Mindread). Little loser (CP2 - Mindread). Furiously out of control, I screamed at him to stay away from the water (CP3 - Shared). I was so mad (CP4 - Insight).

The string of CP5 (Context) sentences drags, and the position of the third one makes it feel like CP5 (Context) rather than CP2 (Mindread). Because of that, the CP4 (Insight) sentence seems to come from nowhere. Nor do the CP2 (Mindread) or CP3 (Shared) sentences deepen characterization or advance the plot. And of course a third person version would exhibit the same problems.

In any point of view, few writers would compose something that clumsy. Yet, at least occasionally, every writer struggles with balancing the CP variables of source, distance, and physicality. Nor is gliding between the CP levels that easy.

But you're apt to find that changing even one sentence can hold the key to repairing the whole faulty paragraph. This revision illustrates how altering the CP levels can sharpen focus and causality:

The clouds were thick, and the Lake Superior beach almost empty (CP5 - Context). I wanted the place to myself, but, as instructed, was watching my little brother build sandcastles (CP3 - Shared). As a wave surged, I bent to pick up a pale pink shell (CP1 - Zoom-in). When I looked up, he was in the water (CP3 - Shared). In the water (CP2 - Mindread)! I ran to him, shrieking till he was more scared than I was (CP3 - Shared).

Often, in the process of trying out a different CP level, you'll discover what was missing and how to correct it. In this case, why she missed her brother testing the waves (the CP1 - Zoom-in sentence), along with the amount of guilt she experienced on seeing him there (the CP2 - Mindread sentence). Again, these changes would pertain to third person in exactly the same way. Altering the CP levels makes this short piece more logical, emotional, even suspenseful.

To revise effectively, you must identify not just what distracts, but why. What do you cover, and how long do you dwell there? The perfect detail, in the wrong place or at the wrong CP level, ceases to be perfect. CP helps you provide what readers need, instead of what happened to enter your mind first.

TIP

Minor changes can produce major differences.

● **How come famous authors get to open however they want?**

Because they're famous! And yet. CP analysis reveals that such novels break fewer "rules" than it seems.

The opening of T. Coraghessan Boyle's *Drop City* exploits the disparity between narrator and character perception. The character introduced here seems to personify naïveté. She feels she's captured all this love and freedom and goodness, the way you might bait your hook and unexpectedly find an absolutely perfect morning dancing on the end of your line.

That's exactly the metaphor Boyle chooses, and that's why his reputation isn't the main hook for this novel. Though the protagonist doesn't infer the irony, a netted fish signals defeat as well as victory. Ebulliently boasting about her unspoiled happiness, the protagonist fails to notice that anything might be amiss.

To make certain that readers notice what the character didn't, the narrator introduces a series of death references—even including a "guillotine." The conflicting narrator versus character language insinuates a harsh awakening for this gullible young woman. And this foreshadowing is the source of tension on the novel's first page.

As the above example demonstrates, the technique of narrator/character contrast can elicit suspense and emotion just as effectively as overt predicament. What hooks readers in such cases? What the character doesn't know.

CP assists with dramatic irony by reminding you of the ingenious and crucial distinction between narrator and character. How can these two play off each other? How can your narrator transcend mere explanation or description?

Used skillfully, setting, too, can build an opening hook. *When the World Was Steady*, by Claire Messud, begins with eight sentences of CP5 (Context) before readers finally meet the protagonist in the third paragraph. Is this a self-indulgent overdose of CP5 (Context), reminiscent of a 19th century novel? No.

Maybe you're wondering about the hook—the source of tension within the first paragraphs? Without the reader knowing it, the protagonist is being meticulously set up—by the setting surrounding her. This isn't just any old setting, either. If description lasts only a paragraph or two, an unfamiliar location like Bali requires minimal justification.

Yet there's something far more arresting occurring in these opening paragraphs. Messud dispenses details about setting to establish the emotional parameters of this world. In Bali, where the novel takes place, it's believed that people find their bearings by identifying their relationship to the mountain chains and their individual peaks. Anyone unable to articulate their relative position is *"palang."* The label suggests that you're not merely stranded: to be adrift in this way is psychologically and spiritually incapacitating. Paralyzing.

That's precisely the emotional state of this protagonist. Messud establishes Emily's predicament so effectively that a mundane choice about whether or not to drink a soda assumes the proportion of dilemma. The CP5 (Context) hooks, exactly as its author intended. The author lays a foundation that generates instant empathy, a useful strategy for a vulnerable protagonist like the one in this novel.

CP can help you analyze technique in any fiction you read, and that will help you decide which levels to choose and how often in your own prose. Once you're comfortable with the fundamentals, consider whether each level fulfills the purpose you intended for it—establishing background, promoting intimacy, providing visuals, and so on. Ultimately, though, every CP level shares the same purpose: deepening the emotional response to the characters.

> **TIP**
>
> Use your narrator to perform familiar tasks in unfamiliar ways.

● **Are transitions between CP levels crucial?**

You bet. CP levels cover different aspects of a character's world, and all of these strands must mesh seamlessly. How does this passage read?

> Herbert tipped his hat to the woman wheeling the stroller (CP1 - Zoom-in). The street was dusty, the sky overcast (CP5 - Context). Little acts of courtesy, of pleasantness (CP2 - Mindread). The wind gusted (CP5 - Context).

The woman reached down to adjust the muffler over the little girl's mouth (CP1 - Zoom-in). He looked up at the sky (CP3 - Shared). Every trace of sunlight had disappeared (CP5 - Context). Where was the pleasantness for him (CP4 - Insight)?

The passage above covers one brief moment in Herbert's stroll. But because the CP levels jolt from internal to external and distant and close, reading this passage is like riding a car that needs new shock absorbers.

But look how easy it is to make a few changes and offer a smooth glide.

Herbert tipped his hat to the woman wheeling the stroller down Fifth Avenue (CP1 - Zoom-in). The carriage left little tracks in the accumulated dust (CP5 - Context). Beneath a sky this overcast, little acts of courtesy, of pleasantness mattered (CP3 - Shared). Just then the wind gusted, and the woman reached down to lovingly adjust the muffler over her little girl's mouth (CP3 - Shared). He felt chilly himself (CP3 - Shared). Where did the sunlight go (CP2 - Mindread)? He wanted some pleasantness of his own (CP4 - Insight). And where was that (CP2 - Mindread)?

The transitions in the second illustration would link foreground to background exactly the same in first person as third. Transitions remain consistent across different points of view, because all of them require unobtrusive connections that propel readers forward without repeating. Rather than randomly depicting one thing after another, progress logically from distant to close, character to narrator, and external to internal.

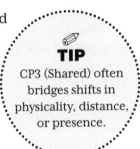

TIP

CP3 (Shared) often bridges shifts in physicality, distance, or presence.

● **Doesn't CP4 (Insight) *tell*?**

Not when you do it right. Telling condescends by explaining the obvious. In contrast, effective CP4 (Insight) clarifies what's not obvious at all.

Dr. Kalinda Mattison resembled no stereotype of any surgeon. No one would compare her with any member of the sex-obsessed cast on "Grey's Anatomy." Neither did she look nor act like a librarian demanding that everyone whisper. Certainly not. This was a woman whose breeding, education, training, and confidence left her free to be exactly herself. Nothing more or less. At thirty-seven, she claimed the self-composure that few achieve before forty-seven. So her infatuation with the guy from food-service astonished her as much as everyone else.

A second illustration of the potential effectiveness of CP4 (Insight) comes from *The Europeans* by Henry James. Eloquently, the narrator probes the character of a character:

> There were several ways of understanding her: there was what she said, and there was what she meant, and there was something between the two, that was neither.

This description is not only illuminating but exquisitely phrased. There's keen observation here, couched in language that forces one to reflect on a meaning that's slightly elusive. Exactly what inhabits the hazy realm between what's "said" and "meant"?

Take the time to examine CP4 (Insight) sentences in both classic and contemporary novels. You'll notice that this level is almost always most effective when it merges the sense of what it reveals with the grace of the wording conveying that meaning. If you can't make a CP4 (Insight) sentence "sound good," this could signal that you need to select a different CP level.

But don't let the necessity of composing effective CP4 (Insight) discourage you from mastering it. Illuminating isn't "telling." Why conflate nuanced interpretation with oversimplified bludgeoning? Abstract judgments such as she's pretty, smart, well-educated, or rich don't demystify characters. Instead, work on both what CP4 (Insight) can reveal and precise language to express that. This is a challenge worth meeting.

> **TIP**
> CP4 (Insight) can provide psychological dimension beyond what cinematic CP1 (Zoom-in) can offer.

● **Do CP4 (Insight) and CP2 (Mindread) blend easily?**

Beautifully, but not easily. CP4 (Insight) is contemplative, while CP2 (Mindread) is uncensored. For completeness, combine them. Yet the tone, pronouns, and verb tense must flow like currents in a single stream, blending analysis with emotion, as the following does:

The narrator (CP4 - Insight) illuminates the protagonist's background, while the CP2 (Mindread) sentences expose fear, anger, and jealousy. Since people are primarily fervent or composed, reality rarely offers this opportunity for both uncensored emotion and temperate analysis of it. The best fiction, however, balances narrator analysis with character discharge.

> **TIP**
> Despite contrasting roles, the narrator and viewpoint character must blend seamlessly.

● **Why does CP2 (Mindread) sometimes sound artificial?**

Formality. Few guys facing guns dispassionately assess the trajectory of unforeseen obstacles. Instead? Sentence fragments. Brutal candor. Like this:

> All her fault. Working late. Meeting clients in the city, Clients, huh? And the house, the money, the yacht, the kids—all go to her? No freaking way. Want to screw around, sweet tart? Let your roadkill support you in the accustomed style. And if you think you deserve the kids with all that whoring around? Think again. Weekends only, and not one penny. Understand?

Only the illusion of complete transparency between reader and character fulfills the intended purpose of CP2 (Mindread). Paranoid people don't think, "So hateful and scary. What'll I do?" To capture the inner self credibly, be blunt. Plumb terror or rage. If there's madness afoot, expose it. Don't hold back.

TIP

CP2 (Mindread) must strip down to bare emotion, yet never clash with the narrator.

● **Does CP2 (Mindread) ever create issues with verb tense and point of view?**

Unfortunately, yes. Many novels are past tense and/or third person, which authors must reconcile with the first person/present tense tone that makes thoughts feel authentic.

Italics or quotation mark for that purpose might look like this:

> Addie sighed (CP1 - Zoom-in). "I want to be with a blue-eyed someone (CP2 - Mindread)," she thought.

> or

> Addie sighed (CP1 - Zoom-in). *I want to be with a blue-eyed someone* (CP2 - Mindread).

Using italics or quotation marks, you can legitimately change the pronoun or verb tense. Yet such sentences often sound at least slightly off-key, and many novelists use quotes and italics inconsistently. Worse till, this kind of formatting distracts. CP2 is the most intimate level, so it's particularly ineffectual to remind readers that they're reading.

An alternative is disguising the verbs and pronouns that cause the inconsistency:

Sentence fragments:

These mimic the disjoined nature of thought while omitting bumps between past tense and present:

> Addie longed for someone with eyes that blue (CP4 - Insight). Such amazing eyes (CP2 - Mindread).

Ambiguous pronouns.

Though "you," "someone," or "who" are technically pronoun shifts from third person, many readers will find the examples below less distracting than the option of quotes or italics:

> Addie longed for someone with eyes that blue (CP4 - Insight). Eyes you could stare at forever (CP2 - Mindread).

or

> Addie longed for someone with eyes that blue (CP4 - Insight). Who wouldn't fall for those eyes (CP2 - Mindread)?

> **TIP**
> In third person point of view, CP2 (Mindread) requires quotes, italics, fragments, or less obvious pronoun case.

● **Why not make everything CP1 (Zoom-in) so readers can reach their own conclusions?**

Because narrators contribute. They illuminate while locating, clarifying, and compressing. How long and tedious would your novel have to be if you presented everything in *live time*? In CP5 (Context), CP4 (Insight), and CP3 (Shared), your narrator shares the burden of communication with your characters.

Many writers, anxious about *telling*, use the narrator as rarely as possible. Though this caution does make some sense, in many instances only the narrator can get the job done. Interpretation and condensation guide readers, while overstatement, abstraction, or oversimplification represent the *telling* that readers definitely don't want. The trick is *telling* only what you can't *show*.

The particular audience for each book affects the response to the narrator's commentary and explanation. For all readers, though, the joy of fiction is the uniqueness of each moment and sentence. Sometimes you want the narrator, sometimes not. The point of CP is sensitivity to whether each moment—each sentence—benefits from narrator, character, or both.

> **TIP**
> Use CP to choose the level that delivers maximum tension, momentum, and emotion.

● **Are there remedies for insufficient external (CP5 - Context and CP1- Zoom-in)?**

1. Introduce gesture and motion. Dry the dishes, call the grandson, pet the dog, fling the pizza. Grab the knife.

2. Convey emotion physically: Babbling, fleeing, grimacing, swigging a martini.

3. Reflect emotion with CP5 (Context). But beware that first kiss beneath a full moon.

4. Add tangible clues to change CP4 (Insight) or CP2 (Mindread) to CP3 (Shared).

5. Read external-oriented works (CP5 - Context and CP1 - Zoom-in), like Tracy Chevalier's *Remarkable Creatures*, Sarah Dunant's *Blood and Beauty*, Richard Powers' *Time of Our Singing*, and Joanna Trollope's *The Spanish Lover*.

● **Are there remedies for insufficient internal (CP4 - Insight and CP2 - Mindread)?**

1. Explore multi-faceted emotions (usually CP4 - Insight).

2. Add metaphor, such as "Alicia resembled a comatose patient on a respirator."

3. Blend in psychology or even a little backstory (usually CP4 - Insight).

4. Change some CP5 (Context) or CP1 (Zoom-in) to CP3 (Shared).

5. Read works emphasizing the internal (CP4 - Insight, CP2 - Mindread), like Chitra Divakaruni's *Queen of Dreams*, Jonathan Franzen's *Purity*, Ian McEwan's *Solar*, and Claire Messud's *The Emperor's Children*.

CP Review

1. Which level should writers omit?

2. Why not start every *scene* or chapter with CP5 (Context)?

3. Which level usually generates the most effective *summaries*?

4. What do details about setting, fact, and theory share in common?

5. What's a shrewd location for CP2 (Mindread) sentences or fragments?

6. What's wrong with "I felt my vision blur" or "She felt her throat tighten"?

7. Which level excludes metaphor?

8. How can CP strengthen crowd *scenes*?

9. In most novels, which two levels occur least frequently?

10. Which levels make dialogue less abstract?

11. How does CP3 (Shared) imitate the way humans think?

12. Which levels might engage readers least?

13. Which level usually produces the greatest tension?

14. Which level fosters momentum?

15. What's an effective device for switching between CP levels?

Answers

1. None. Though in varying amounts, fiction needs all five levels.

2. Setting often lacks conflict, so CP3 (Shared) frequently hooks more successfully.

3. *Collapsed time* benefits from the emotion and thus empathy that CP3 (Shared) often adds.

4. They're all CP5 (Context). Without individual characters, this most distant level can mimic nonfiction and often relies on voice or vividness to spice it up.

5. After dialogue. That's a great place to contrast speech with ironic thought.

6. That's "feeling a feeling." Whether third person or first, just "blur" or "tighten."

7. Metaphor can appear in any level, but is most infrequent in CP1 (Zoom-in).

8. Intersperse other levels with CP5 (Context) to create immediacy within panorama.

9. CP5 (Context) and CP2 (Mindread) are respectively rather distant or emotional and thus tend to appear least often. It's usually best to avoid more than two or three consecutive sentences in either level.

10. CP5 (Context), CP3 (Shared), and CP1 (Zoom-in) provide tangibility.

11. By capturing the hard-wired instinct to draw conclusions from external cues.

12. CP5 (Context) and CP4 (Insight) can distance readers from the characters, while CP2 (Mindread) can belabor the obvious.

13. CP3 (Shared) raises stakes by combining character behavior with narrator perception.

14. CP1 (Zoom-in) lets readers experience *scenes* as characters do—without filter.

15. Dialogue can ease shifts between CP levels.

> **TIP**
> CP promotes dispassionate assessment of what's included, omitted, or emphasized.

☞ **Exercise**: Originating with CP

Choose a paragraph from your novel that dissatisfies you and change the CP level of **every** sentence.

☞ **Exercise**: Gliding between Narrator and Character

Select a passage from your novel where both narrator and characters deepen a *scene* yet don't seem to share it—almost as if they compete with each other. Revise to make their separate contributions and voices contribute to a unified flow.

☞ **Exercise**: Breaking Habits with CP

Model a paragraph of your own after the CP levels in a passage you love.

☞ **Exercise**: Revising with CP

Part a.) Assign a CP number to each sentence in either the first person or third person version of the passage below. The sentences are numbered so you can match them to the answers, though, again, note that certain sentences are open to interpretation.

Third Person point of view

Books covered almost every inch of the store (1). Marjorie resented having only forty minutes here (2). This seemed a good day to help herself to another paperback (3). After carefully scanning the room, she slipped a small one into her huge purse (4). Marjorie raised her head (5). She decided things looked okay (6). She'd always felt that stealing books is like stealing bread (7). After all, it's a fact that few children learn to read at four (8) But if dad knew what she was doing, he'd never forgive her (9).

After checking whether she had enough time, Marjorie grabbed a book and started reading (10). She wasn't in the mood for the philosophy of science , though (11). She headed for the art section (12). A man in a drab gray suit fell in step behind her (13). Looking disgusted, he tapped her shoulder and pointed at her purse (14). The tears poured out (15). Now she'd lost another bookstore forever (16).

First person point of view

Books covered almost every inch of the store (1). I resented having only forty minutes here (2). This seemed a good day to help myself to another paperback (3). After carefully scanning the room, I slipped a small book into my huge purse (4). I raised my head (5). I decided things looked okay (6). I've always felt that stealing books is like stealing bread (7). After all, it's a fact that few children learn to read at four (8). But if dad knew what I was doing, he'd never forgive me (9).

After checking whether I had enough time, I grabbed a book and started reading (10). I wasn't in the mood for the philosophy of science , though (11). I headed for the art section (12). A man in a drab gray suit fell in step behind me (13). Looking disgusted, he tapped my shoulder and pointed at my purse (14). The tears poured out (15). Now I've lost another bookstore forever (16).

CP levels for either version of the two paragraphs above:

1. CP5 - Context	9. CP4 - Insight
2. CP4 - Insight	10. CP 3 -Shared
3. CP4 - Insight	11. CP4 - Insight
4. CP 3 -Shared	12. CP1 - Zoom-in
5. CP1 - Zoom-in	13. CP1 - Zoom-in
6. CP4 - Insight	14. CP3 - Shared
7. CP4 - Insight	15. CP1 - Zoom-in
8. CP5 - Context	16. CP4 - Insight

Part b) In either the first or third person version above, change the CP level of each sentence. After completing this, you might want to compare it with the versions below.

A CP Revision:

Third person point of view

At the sight of books covering almost every inch of the store, Marjorie exhaled loudly (CP3 - Shared). Forty minutes—so little time, so many books (CP2 - Mindread). Furtively, she slipped a small paperback into her huge purse (CP3 - Shared). Then she raised her head, scanning the room (CP1 - Zoom-in). Looked okay (CP2 - Mindread). Some people steal books the way others steal bread (CP5 - Context). She'd felt this way since she learned to read at four (CP4 - Insight) But dad would freak (CP2 - Minded).

After checking her watch, Marjorie grabbed a book and started reading (CP1 - Zoom-in). No philosophy of science today, though (CP2 - Mindread). Focused on reaching the art section in the short lunch hour remaining, she never saw the man in the drab gray suit fall in step behind her (CP3 - Shared). He tapped her shoulder and pointed at her purse (CP1 - Zoom-in). She couldn't help tearing up (CP3 - Shared). Another bookstore gone forever (CP2 - Mindread).

First person point of view

At the sight of books covering almost every inch of the store, I exhaled loudly (CP3 - Shared). Forty minutes—so little time, so many books (CP2 - Mindread). Furtively, I slipped a small paperback into my huge purse (CP 3 - Shared). Then I raised my head, scanning the room (CP1 - Zoom-in). Looked okay (CP2 - Mindread). Some people steal books the way others steal bread (CP5 - Context). I've felt this way since I learned to read at four (CP4 - Insight) But dad would freak (CP2 - Mindread).

After checking my watch, I grabbed a book and started reading (CP1 - Zoom-in). No philosophy of science today, though (CP2 - Mindread). Focused on reaching the art section in the short lunch hour remaining, I never saw the man in the drab gray suit fall in step behind me (CP3 - Shared). He tapped my shoulder and pointed at my purse (CP1 - Zoom-in). I couldn't help tearing up (CP3 - Shared). Another bookstore gone forever (CP2 - Mindread).

And so...

CP is an effective revision tool. Its numbers not only promote objective assessment of your manuscript, but from an unconventional perspective. You can view your manuscript from a different angle now, and that's an opportunity for fresh solutions to any problems that diagnosis revealed. Can you raise the stakes by presenting this moment from narrator instead of character, or the reverse? Is a passage sluggish because it overdoes one CP variable at the expense of the others?

This kind of sensitivity won't materialize effortlessly. In any area, new skills develop from analysis combined with practice. So give CP a try. Experiment with transforming CP5 (Context) into CP1 (Zoom-in). Make a CP4 (Insight) into a CP3 (Shared). The more you apply CP—either deliberately or just in the back of your mind—the more swiftly and flexibly you'll implement what the system offers. CP helps revise suspense, balance, and pace.

Once you're better at assessing and improving the choice and placement of details, it's time to scrutinize the sentences that build *scene and summary*. Since sentences do lots of work, they deserve lots of work. The quality of your sentences affects the acuity of your perception, which, in turn, produces sentences of greater precision and beauty. Sentences with melody, meaning, and momentum.

Are there techniques for varying, smoothing, and emphasizing while capturing causality? Coming right up...

Deep Revision
Tip # 8
Diagnosing weaknesses is the first step toward repairing them.

9

"Sexy" Syntax

Getting It On

Myth No one has time to revise every sentence, and readers don't expect it, anyway.

Of course they do. In a novel, syntax, or sentence structure, deflates or elevates humor, tension, and most everything else. Still doubt whether every sentence matters? Consider this dental office sign:

> Should you floss all your teeth every day?
>
> Just the ones you want to keep.

Should all your sentences be good? Just the ones you want to keep.

> ✎
> **TIP**
> Sentence structure
> strengthens story
> structure.

Perhaps you think in interminable sentences or enjoy interpreting them. Despite that, few readers tolerate lumbering or bewildering prose. To grasp the effect of such issues, picture momentum as a tire hurtling down a hill; every distraction halts progress. Deposit enough pebbles, and the tire scarcely moves.

What piles up pebbles? Repetition, self-consciousness, extra words or details, and graceless constructions. Verbose, stiff, or impenetrable sentences don't merely irritate—they bury the prose that evokes a small smile of pride.

Besides, attention to sentences yields insight that the *thesaurus syndrome* can never produce. Unless you know exactly what you want to say, how beautifully can you say it?

Once again, you want a view from another angle. Most writers notice either the big picture or the individual words. Attention to syntax falls between these, offering an alternative way to assess your manuscript. Restructure your awkward sentences, and you'll generate smooth passages that convey your surprising new discoveries about plot and character.

> ✎
> **TIP**
> Vague conception
> generates vague
> expression.

Verbs Do It

Unlike other words, many verbs propel: "stagger," "butcher," "bulldoze," "sneer." What else? "Delineate," "photosynthesize," "reminisce," "calculate," "mortify," or "enunciate." They photograph and haunt, transforming the static nature of language into the dynamic nature of life. Mark Twain wasn't kidding about "When you catch an adjective, kill it."

Yet he then added that adjectives contribute when separated from each other, and obviously, novels need every part of speech. Still, why make the engine driving your story lug extra weight? Nancy can smile sympathetically instead of offering a sympathetic smile. "Took a quick look at" can't rival "peeked." Perhaps a word like "feral" delights you. Can that truly justify "was feeling feral"?

TIP

Any word that can be a verb should be.

Passive versus Active

It's a truth universally acknowledged by most people that passive voice is disliked by them. Contrast "The gun was brandished by Tammi" with "Tammi brandished the gun." That first sentence highlights an inanimate object, and novel readers follow characters, not objects.

Tammi, the psychological subject, must be the grammatical one, so she can act rather than be acted upon. Misplaced emphasis adds words and drains immediacy. Consider these: "There weren't so many ways for Rapunzel to escape," or "No was hated more by Captain Hook than Peter Pan."

You're probably groaning. Since no one wants readers doing that, why is passive voice prevalent? Habit. Academia. A magnetic noun or adjective.

Can't make a sentence active? Maybe you're a little fuzzy on what you want to say. Or maybe you don't need that sentence at all?

TIP

A search for "by," "there are," and "it is" identifies many passive sentences so you can fix or delete them.

Yet in certain circumstances, passive voice is the best option:

● **Tone.**

"The reports of my death are greatly exaggerated." Mark Twain would've deadened the humor with "They've greatly exaggerated reports of my death."

● **Emphasis.**

"Attention must be paid" is the most famous line in Arthur Miller's *Death of a Salesman*. "We must pay attention to him," though, would go as unnoticed as Willie Loman himself.

● **Rhythm.**

Cadence sometimes justifies extra words.

TIP

Choose passive voice intentionally instead of inadvertently.

Auxiliaries and Other Anti-Active Verbs

The helping verbs make the dynamic ones haul excess weight. Avoid these whenever possible:

Is	Has	Could
Be	Have	Shall
Am	Had	Should
Are	Do	Will
Was	Does	Would
Were	Did	Must
Been	Can	

Besides, what's worse at the end of a sentence than a helping verb is?

All weak verbs distance readers from the characters. Why say "Eric began to watch" instead of "Eric watched"? Eliminate distracting set ups like "was starting to," "considered leaving," "wondered if she should," "hoped that he could," or "imagined that they would." Substitute "completed" for "planned to complete" and "lusted" for "underwent a sensation of lust." "Ann felt rage" instead of "Ann fumed" equals Ann "feeling a feeling"—and readers feeling little.

Like weak verbs, those requiring prepositions distance readers from the action. Replace "was opposed to," "appealed to," "recovered from," "intended to," "cluttered up," and so on. Not tighten up. Tighten.

Exercise: Harnessing Verbs

Check your manuscript for nouns or adjectives that could be verbs. Mobilize them.

TIP
Weak verbs waste words.

Verbs Make Love

Verbs tease and tantalize. They dazzle, darken edges, and drizzle sensuality. Exercise them. Reduce flabby syntax. Better still, metaphorical verbs capture the complex, ephemeral nature of emotion.

Some Metaphorical Verbs

Bombard	Hoard
Bud	Hurl
Collapse	Illuminate
Cut	Nourish
Decimate	Rub
Devour	Scour
Digest	Spoon-feed
Disintegrate	Sugar-coat
Embark	Swallow
Ferret	Weasel

Yet metaphorical verbs can spell treachery. Eloise can't plan to tread lightly because swimming through troubled waters rattles her. Mismatched verbs torpedo the metaphor deep in the soil, disrupting the harvest. Watch what you set up. For example, the words themselves never "cower," "bridle," or "submit." Warmth doesn't bloom on Babette's arm where Mark casually touched her. Verbs that personify often irritate most: stars that grin, trees that teach, flowers that hurry toward bloom. Readers who cower.

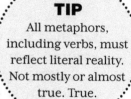

TIP
All metaphors, including verbs, must reflect literal reality. Not mostly or almost true. True.

Clarity at the Sentence Level

The *thesaurus syndrome* is easy! Fun! Often, though, it improves an individual word while leaving the overall meaning blurry. Does each sentence articulate your intention? Belong where you put it? Sentences help readers understand—or not.

Wordiness obstructs comprehension. Despite the hope that additional words or details foster precision, the opposite is usually true. Clutter buries while somehow feeling simultaneously frantic and tedious.

Start with removing any excess, because this simplifies both structural and syntactical revision. Next, ground the abstract with imagery. Let your characters *show* what you struggled to *tell*.

Next, consider grammar. If you never "got" it—in either sense, don't bother now with diagramming sentences or differentiating technical categories. Do familiarize yourself, however, with the basics. This protects you against "Although ashamed of what he'd done, the poop got banished to Rover's kennel."

Learn a few "rules" in order to consciously decide when to break them. Grammar highlights problems not just with agreement, but also with complexity and vague or misplaced modifiers. For example:

> In his mind, Salvatore refused to let Francine continue, admonished her recklessness with threats of expulsion from the restaurant, until he reminded himself there was no restaurant, save for the open space and the two of them who were cloistered there.

The phrase "in his mind" redundantly states the obvious, and "restaurant" appears twice. How many other words could one rephrase or cut? Next, parallel ideas demand parallelism, but what's the relationship between "refused to let" and "admonished," or any of the other verbs here? Finally, this might require two sentences.

A little grammar and a lot of close reading, perhaps aloud, identify bloated or unintelligible clauses or phrases. "Eva was amused that the dinner she hadn't wanted to attend wasn't a total pleasure for her husband." Who wants to reread sentences to decipher their meaning? Grammar helps you see what your reader does.

But, as with passive voice, exceptions exist. For instance, you usually need the word "and" in a list like "aqua, serpentine, jewel-encrusted." But use the word "and" imprecisely with clauses, and you get "Ann swallowed, and the sun shone." What?

When logical, it's fine to start sentences with "and," "or," "yet," "but," "nor," "because." and "so." Opening with a conjunction like "because" won't necessarily produce a fragment, and, in any case, novelists get to use fragments, though sparingly.

∞ **Exercise:** Applying Grammar

Select a disappointing sentence from your novel and analyze its structure. Does it bulge with numerous clauses, phrases, or compound subjects and verbs? Use grammar to improve that sentence. Repeat as needed. The more you practice, the more smoothly and swiftly you'll compose strong sentences. Almost automatically.

TIP
Grammar is the why behind "it doesn't sound right."

Energy at the Sentence Level

Make your syntax as dynamic as the world it captures. That means starting sentences in different ways. Utilize phrases like "From the window," or clauses like "Since Ben's betrayal." Although syntax should reflect action or tranquility, a long string of short sentences jolts. Mix it up. Like this:

> My love for Linton is like the foliage in the woods: time will change it, I'm well aware, as winter changes the trees. My love for Heathcliff resembles the eternal rocks beneath: a source of little visible delight, but necessary. Nelly, I am Healthcliff! He's always, always in my mind: not as a pleasure, any more than I am always a pleasure to myself, but as my own being. —Emily Brontë, *Wuthering Heights*

The first sentence of the paragraph above dips to a low point with the words "time will change it, I'm well aware..." There's another downward turn with "but necessary." Then the insistent rhythm begins to climb again. The paragraph has only one short sentence. That's the crucial one, where the protagonist identifies with the antagonist. They are one and the same.

Imagine this passage without this particular juxtaposition of patterns: self versus world, love for one man versus another, repetition of "always," and crisp identification of what is and what is not. The source of power here, as in so much writing, is contrast.

Regardless of genre, with some practice, you can create appealing patterns yourself. Choose smooth sounds, then oppose them with harsh ones. Vary the sentence length (long or short) and also the type of sentence (simple, compound, complex, question, fragment).

Play with rhythm, too. This last option is both trickiest and most effective. Unless you establish rhythmic expectations first, how can you disrupt or punctuate them? So take some time to examine rhythm in fiction you love. Novelists can gain much from scrutinizing sentence structure in both classic and contemporary works. Consider modeling some of your own sentences after those that impress you.

When you're collecting sentences, notice that rhythm builds from variety in structure. If most of your sentences are either simple or compound, you're trying to create a kaleidoscope with only reds and blues instead of the full color range.

Use all the syntactical tools at your disposal. Watch yourself grow increasingly comfortable with them all the time. Because not even the best plot can entirely disguise prose that takes too long or sounds too familiar. Vary habitual patterns like: "Ann ordered pizza. Mark wanted the fish. Eloise had salad." The reader yawned. This also applies to "Dabbing on eye shadow, Ann...," "Knotting his tie, Alan..." and "Lulling the reader..."

TIP

Build patterns. Afterwards? Break them.

Doing It More Than Once

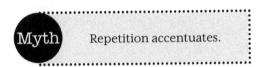

Myth Repetition accentuates.

Most of the time, repetition bores, so any doubling must be deliberate.

●◆ **Doubling**: Duplicating information, verbs, dialogue, or general and specific versions.

Why have "Ella grab and tug," or "Herbert turn and leave"? Must Tom choke with rage immediately before balling his hands into fists? This goes for metaphor, too. Choose one you needn't explain, or you wind up duplicating the literal and symbolic versions.

Even subtle repetition slows momentum. Consider this:

> With only three years in the United States, Wilhemina spoke rudimentary English. She often mixed pronouns and omitted articles, forcing her audience to mentally edit her sentences while listening.

No need to mention both "rusty English" (general) and its manifestation (specific), or to add "while listening" to "mentally edit." Say it right the first time.

Novelists repeat partly because real conversation involves thinking aloud, offering both specific and general, and *telling* and *showing* the same detail. To illustrate:

> "I wish you would stop leaving the milk out on the counter," Thomas said.

"I left the milk out on the counter because ..."

But fiction isn't conversation. Avoid *doubling*. This includes bringing characters up to date. If your readers know what happened, use *summary*. Don't repeat in *real time*.

TIP

Twice isn't twice as good.

☞**Exercise:** Breaking habits

List three sentence habits you want to change. Possibilities might include:

• Passive voice

• Word repetition, whether noun, pronoun, or preposition

• Inscrutable constructions ("The number of times that spiders scared her meant...")

• Persistent patterns (e.g. subject, verb, and object)

• Jargon or "abstruse" words

• Verbs requiring prepositions

• Inadvertent grammatical errors

Choose one of these, and keep it in mind as you revise. You'll probably improve faster if you tackle one issue at a time instead of diving into everything simultaneously.

☞**Exercise:** Typing as Teaching

No magic formula insures strong sentences, and be skeptical about anyone claiming otherwise. The trick is developing greater sensitivity to language. Read some good stuff, and notice why you consider it good.

Hunter S. Thompson famously typed Hemingway and Fitzgerald—to have the experience of typing a great novel. Want to type a passage from a novel you admire? Go for it. Here's a passage to get you started:

The long stretches of the waterway ran on, deserted, into the gloom of overshadowed distances. On silvery sandbanks hippos and alligators sunned themselves side by side. The broadening waters flowed through a mob of wooded islands; you lost your way on that river as you would in a desert, and butted all day long against shoals, trying to find the channel, till you thought yourself bewitched and cut off forever from everything you had known once—somewhere far away in another existence perhaps. There were moments when one's past came back to one, as it will sometimes when you have not a moment to spare to yourself; but it came in the shape of an unrestful and noisy dream, remembered with wonder amongst the overwhelming realities of this strange world of plants, and water, and silence. And this stillness of life did not in the least resemble a peace. It was the stillness of an implacable force brooding over an inscrutable intention. It looked at you with a vengeful aspect. —Joseph Conrad, *Heart of Darkness*

TIP

Powerful, haunting sentences build powerful, haunting novels.

Causality at the Sentence Level

Myth

Cause and effect pertains only to plot.

Every aspect of fiction affects every other. The connectors between *scenes*, paragraphs, and sentences either obscure or accentuate causality.

Connector: A *summary*, transition, conjunction, or conjunctive adverb linking a moment, detail, location, or motive with what follows.

If you eliminate *connectors*, you get this:

Sue made her way to the kitchen. She wanted a glass of water. Her husband tiptoed out of her sister's bedroom. The loose board creaked.

versus

Sue left the kitchen **where** she'd gone for a drink of water. **While** her husband tiptoed out of his sister-in-law's bedroom, that loose board creaked **again**.

The first version lurches from detail to detail, isolating events and omitting fluidity, sequence, and foreshadowing. In contrast, *connectors* build plot from a series of stills:

Although Max tiptoes, Sue catches him. **Because** she learns the truth, she'll souse the louse.

The interaction between Sue and Max warrants confrontation **now** rather than **yesterday** or **often**. Certain *connectors* shift immediacy (CP1- Zoom-in) to ongoing time (CP3 - Shared).

Some *connectors* that dilute *live time* include

Always	Every (dawn, night, etc.)
Constantly	Frequently
Continually	Often
Daily	Time after time
Each (time, day, etc.)	Usually

TIP

Connectors assign correspondence, sequence, or consequence.

The choices from the list above usually create *summary*. In contrast, *connectors* like "now," "instantly," or "abruptly" escalate drama within *scene*.

Without *connectors*, every sentence is isolated from every other:

Mady stuck out her Kool-Aid-colored tongue. Dad offered the Mickey Mouse toothbrush.

Prose needs *connectors*. But choose an illogical one, and you get:

Mady stuck out her Kool-Aid-colored tongue, <u>and</u> her Dad has red hair.

The word "and" conveys equivalence, even when that makes no sense. Equivalent *connectors* like "and" also slow momentum. The run-on structure of this and this and this produces:

Mady giggled with pleasure and she danced around in delight and Dad waved the toothbrush in the air over her head and they chased each other and both were extremely happy.

Run-on and weak compound sentences undermine cause and effect by equating everything. Reserve compound sentences for moments of equivalence, like

Mady giggled with pleasure, and Dad kept tickling until she was practically breathless.

But equivalence isn't always what you need. To capture progression, choose sequential *connectors*:

> **After** Mady stuck out her Kool-Aid-colored tongue, Dad offered the Mickey Mouse toothbrush.

Sequence marks time, but not causality. For that you need another kind of *connector*:

> **Though** Mady stuck out her Kool-Aid-colored tongue, Dad didn't offer the Mickey Mouse toothbrush.

When plausible, choose causal *connectors* like "because," since these capture motivation while escalating wonder and worry. It's more difficult to achieve emphasis like that with *connectors* that reflect equality ("and"), temporality ("usually"), or sequence ("after").

But since every type of *connector* serves a different purpose, you need to select the one apt for each situation, because each will differ from every other. With a little practice, you'll make these choices more and more instinctively.

Equalize with *connectors* like "and," "again," "also."

Measure with *connectors* like "before," "later," "when."

Signal ongoing time with *connectors* like "always," "frequently," "rarely."

Identify condition with *connectors* like "if," "but," "although."

Express causality with *connectors* like "because," "since," "otherwise."

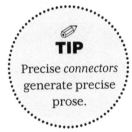

TIP
Precise *connectors* generate precise prose.

The *Connector* Connection

Neither genre nor point of view affects connectors. Here's a first person illustration:

> **After** that day, I would **never** go near the pond. **Usually**, I played in the cellar, the apple trees, **even** the dark alley behind the garage, **wherever** I wanted. **Before** the incident my mother **constantly** warned me: "Don't do this **and** forget about doing that." **Now** she said nothing. **So every** day **after** school, I inched closer **and** closer to greater danger.

Changing point of view to omniscient or third limited wouldn't affect any of the words linking the sentences above. Imagine, though, how bumpy the above passage—or one in third limited or omniscient—would sound without the connectors accentuating life before the pond incident and after.

Connectors must bridge one sentence or moment sleekly to the next. Also, the different types of connector must fulfill their respective purposes, such as sequence ("after"), negation ("never"), location ("wherever"), or causality ("so").

For smooth flow, choose the right connector for the many instances when you need one.

The following compiles many *connectors* useful in fiction, intentionally omitting possibilities novelists should probably avoid, like "consequently," "meanwhile," "moreover," "thus," "hitherto," and "therefore."

> **TIP**
> *Connectors* let you communicate more than one kind of time within a single paragraph.

After	If	Rarely	Tomorrow
Afterwards	Immediately	Regularly	Too
Although	Instantly	Repeatedly	Ultimately
As	Instead	Scarcely	Unexpectedly
Because	Less	Seldom	Unless
Before	Likewise	Since	Until
Besides	More	So	Usually
But	Mostly	Sometimes	When
Either	Nearly	Soon	Whenever
Equally	Neither	Still	Where
Eventually	Never	Subsequently	Whether
Finally	Nor	Suddenly	While
Frequently	Not	Surprisingly	Yesterday
Further	Often	Than	Yet
Generally	Once	That	
Gradually	Only	Then	
Hourly	Or	Therefore	
How	Partially	Though	
However	Potentially	Till	

> **TIP**
> Pay attention to *connectors*—so readers needn't.

☞**Exercise:** Adding Causality to Sentences

Check the *connectors* on a random page of your novel. Do they accurately reflect sequence and causality? Do any misuse equivalence? Apply your discoveries throughout.

Musicality at the Sentence Level

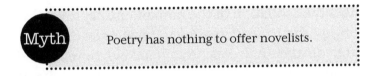

Myth   Poetry has nothing to offer novelists.

Originally, plot and poetry intertwined, and the best fiction preserves this legacy. Rhythm, variety, and echo orchestrate not just poetry, but prose. Some writers sense this intuitively; "That's a pretty sentence," or, "Ugh, that isn't."

Did you get a green thumb and no ear? Don't be discouraged. Read aloud. Notice haunting or ghastly syntax in novels, articles, poems, and websites. The more you sensitize your ear, the sooner you'll compose lovely sentences of your own.

Though you can't go beyond imitating the rhythmic and grammatical structure of your best finds, you can train your ear by analyzing beautiful prose wherever you encounter it.

Which techniques suit your voice and genre? Experiment. Start with analyzing rhythm. You might examine the opening of Peter Benchley's *Jaws*. There, like a shark disturbing the calm, syntax reinforces the relentless advance of danger.

When the words really work, you can speak volumes with only a scant handful. Mark Twain ends *Eve's Diary* with Adam standing at her grave, saying, "Wherever she was, there was Eden." How could any single sentence express more?

But that evasive quality we call "voice" transcends individual components like compression, or even rhythm. How can you go far enough for originality without descending into overkill? Every novelist must balance neutral versus ostentatious, self-indulgent versus spunky. While bludgeoning produces skimming, tedium produces renunciation of a particular book. Withhold every judgment, and you might block the electricity that gives a narrator personality and a novel its voice.

Voice comes less from individual contributions than the synthesis of them all operating in unison, interacting with and influencing each other. Still, parallelism is a great place to start playing with language, because the construction of parallelism involves diction, content, and grammatical structure.

Consider the impact of parallelism in this excerpt from Mark Twain's *The Mysterious Stranger*:

Cain did his murder with a club; the Hebrews did their murders with javelins and swords; the Greeks and Romans added protective armor and the fine arts of military organization and generalship; the Christian has added guns and gunpowder; a few centuries from now he will have so greatly improved the deadly effectiveness of his weapons of slaughter that all men will confess that without Christian civilization war must have remained a poor and trifling thing to the end of time.

The syntax echoes the escalation of the human instinct toward violence. The verb forms graduate from low-key to an increasingly appalling level. The passage accelerates: "did his murder," and "did their murders." A shift follows. Now it's "added," "has added," and "will have so greatly improved." This swelling litany triumphantly climaxes in the ultimate irony of "will confess." The power of the diction and rhythm keep this indictment of humanity fresh and vital, although Mark Twain composed drafts of this work from 1897 through 1908.

Word choice similarly energizes the following excerpt from Charles Dickens, even though he's generally associated with mastery of plot and characterization. Like Mark Twain's passage, the power of the following originates in the resonance between ideas and the expression of them:

The water of the fountain ran, the swift river ran, the day ran into evening, so much life in the city ran into death according to rule, time and tide waited for no man, the rats were sleeping close together in their dark holes again, the Fancy Ball was lighted up at supper, all things ran their course. —*A Tale of Two Cities*

The repetition of "ran"—clearly deliberate rather than unintentional—unifies a passage that covers great breadth. Everything is running, suggesting the impossibility of stopping any manifestation of it.

Dickens also includes a little twist to the proverb "time and tide waited for no man," creating a memorable quote of his own: "all things ran their course." You, too, can use a conventional saying to build a new structure from a tired one, a technique which delights many readers familiar with the original.

Again, contrast is always a useful technique. Here, it invigorates evocation of the landscape: the artificial fountain versus the river, day versus night. In some ways this paragraph seems to describe an entirely normal world. And that's the horror. Who could forget the proximity of the slumbering rats to the illuminated Ball?

Invest some time in studying novelists with glorious voices. The list would be far too lengthy to complete here, but consider some of the following: Sarah Dunant, Chad

Harback, Jean Hanff Korelitz, Hilary Mantel, Toni Morrison, and Amy Tan. Why not continue building your own list of glorious voices?

Many of the glorious voices you identify might be lyrical ones. Of course fiction and poetry are very different genres. As a novelist, how poetic do you get to be? That depends on your audience and your voice. But poetry can add a great deal, as this next example illustrates:

> A day of dappled seaborne clouds.
>
> The phrase and the day and the scene harmonised in a chord. Words. Was it their colours? He allowed them to glow and fade, hue after hue: sunrise gold, the russet and green of apple orchards, azure of waves, the greyfringed fleece of clouds. No, it was not their colours: it was the poise and balance of the period itself. Did he then love the rhythmic rise and fall of words better than their associations of legend and colour? Or was it that, being as weak of sight as he was shy of mind, he drew less pleasure from the reflection of the glowing sensible world through the prism of a language manycoloured and richly storied than from the contemplation of an inner world of individual emotions mirrored perfectly in a lucid supple periodic prose? —James Joyce, *Portrait of the Artist as a Young Man*

This passage opens with the synesthesia of language and landscape translated into sound: a "chord." Everything the protagonist describes is dynamically in flux; the colors shift, and those of the external landscape evoke those of the imagination. Past and present, internal and external merge, because everything in this passage is about the relationship between the artist and his world.

Far ahead of his time, Joyce takes the sort of risks you'd see in writers like Italo Calvino, Cormac McCarthy, Zadie Smith, or David Foster Wallace, just to name a few. And like many of those experimental writers, the gorgeous wording of this passage conveys the questions that many writers face today, whether their work is experimental or not.

The composing of a novel isn't merely a matter of technique, but, on some level, of imagining what it means to compose a novel. Joyce introduces a lot of that musing in this one paragraph written early in his career. Is the visible world the most enticing one? Or perhaps it's the patterns of the words used to articulate that world. And finally, without the words for expression, how could anyone explain vision or feeling?

This is a lot to grasp. Joyce helps out by unifying sound and sense. He offers a *scene*, something to visualize, while the protagonist ruminates on these huge questions. In this monologue, the world itself comes to us through the language capturing it: the rhythmic "rise and fall" and the colors that "glow and fade" in succession.

TIP
Subtle musicality makes prose poetic.

Is "lucid supple periodic prose" our only way to see? To speak? Perhaps it's enough to ask such questions rather than hoping to answer them. But it couldn't hurt for every fiction writer to at least reflect on this.

Of course novelists can overdo stylistic devices. Especially with prose, rhythm must be subtle and further not only sound, but meaning. Avoid the temptation to achieve rhythm with clutter. That includes repetition, filler like "just" and "very," and prepositions that weaken the verbs they complete.

Writers write for different readers, who'll have differing expectations about rhythm, contrast, accent, and music. Without lots of effort, few writers are lucky enough to produce prose that flows effortlessly. Begin with noticing the sound of the sentence—the sentences everywhere. That'll help you hear your own.

TIP
Sleek sentences sound sexy.

Increase skill at managing verbs, grammar, patterns, and echoes. Start now, and you'll soon achieve the effect you want.

∞ Exercise: Revising for Rhythm

Pattern a sentence after one you particularly like. Practice expanding individual phrases and clauses. Eventually you won't need any sort of pattern as a starting point.

✔ Checklist Exercise: Evaluating Your Syntax

☐ Do any sentences in your novel sound flat? Off-key?

☐ Does each sentence reflect the pacing you want?

☐ Do any sentences distract because they're awkward or interminable?

☐ Want to change any passive sentences to active?

☐ Does each sentence emphasize what matters?

☐ Do the verbs entice?

☐ Are your *connectors* present and logical?

☐ Is any repetition intentional and subtle?

☐ Do you vary sentence length and patterns?

☐ Do all the characters sound similar?

☐ Have you repaired preposition overload?

- ☐ Have you omitted the clichés that irritate like ants at a picnic?

- ☐ Do you reflect equivalence with meaningful, beautiful, and memorable parallelism?

- ☐ Have you evaluated both the sound and placement of your sentences?

- ☐ Can you justify every word?

- ☐ Does the quality of your language surprise you?

And so...

Monotony annoys. Clumsiness and wordiness distract. And sequence? Causality? *Connectors* like "after" or "because" delineate relationships and foreshadow consequences. Clear thinking creates sentences that illuminate the novel's world first for the writer, then for the reader.

Whatever you read, notice eloquent sentences and the *connectors* linking them. When you evaluate your own work, identify trouble spots and patiently fix them. Revise and revise. Revise.

Yet excessive rigor can stifle voice. If the voice feels false, can the story feel true? A novel must evolve as an organic structure, or it'll never evolve at all. Sentences resemble the entrances, turrets, and moats of a sand castle at the beach. The best castles often arise spontaneously. So listen to the waves. Play. Make words as dispensable as the sand against the tide. Your own words!

The language and sentences that compose voice originate less from mind than heart. And soul. Ironically, voice merges two opposites: Attention to every rule about storytelling versus a pure naiveté apparently oblivious to constraint or rule. Voice never heard a single one and wouldn't care if it did. It's next.

Deep Revision Tip
#9
Some sentences are beyond repair. For better results, start from scratch.

Voice

or Making Love to and with Your Novel

> **Myth**   Voice is something you have or don't.

Not exactly, though you do release rather than rework voice. That's because readers instinctively detect self-consciousness. So don't try to sound Dickensian or clever. Don't even try to sound like yourself. Don't try, period.

Effort alone won't transform the listless or strained into a sound artless as the sea licking the beach. What's the best strategy for enticing voice out of hiding? Let the characters act and the narrator guide. That puts you the author where you belong: offstage.

Training the Voice

● **Does a writer have more than one voice?**

Yes and no. Voice differs from author to narrator to each character and often from book to book. But certain idiosyncrasies remain constant. No one would mistake Toni Morrison's voice for Jane Austen's.

● **Can writers take voice lessons the way singers do?**

Sort of. Brainstorm. Identify habits in order to discard undesirable ones. Shake things up. Change the CP level. Want other alternatives? Look through the lenses of dilemma, emotion, or sentence sound.

Dig deep into idea and image, plot and character. Down there you'll uncover the unexpected, whether with psychology, patterns, or parallels. Escape the familiar into a world where you notice—and thus articulate—what only you perceive.

Evaluate your novel's deep structure, including the probability of each arc. Are they causal? Could any be more so? Do you inflict dilemma, and is the ending earned? When you transform the unlikely into the plausible, you revolutionize not only plot but language. The energy that electrifies voice originates there.

● **Can you counteract the defensiveness and self-consciousness that dampen voice?**

Only with brutal honesty. Both skill and attitude affect revision. Are you showing off your research? Sharing your pet peeves? Padding instead of plotting? Letting the language of fiction overwhelm the fiction itself?

> **TIP**
> Make the discoveries that only you can. The words will follow.

Ego is both the source of voice and its worst enemy. Never let self supplant story. When a novel has a great voice, it's the narrator's. Don't you want a narrator you needn't hide?

● **Should you be true to yourself or your readers?**

Both, of course. Respect your unique vocal personality. At the same time, respect your readers by offering clarity, momentum, transitions, and so on. Attention to audience bolsters confidence, because the focus becomes delivering the book rather than any fantasies about it. Or any doubts. Being other-directed often elicits the best in everything. Including voice.

● **Can questions contribute to your fiction?**

Absolutely. An occasional question accentuates, varies pace, subdues formality, and captures character thought. All of those can potentially amplify tension.

● **To protect voice, should you pour out the first draft as fast and freely as you can?**

Maybe not. Sometimes the only way to discover what doesn't work is to create redundant sentences, false plot points, and faltering *scenes*. Here's the problem, though. Novelists often waste time trying to repair weak material instead of conceiving better options. Unless you can cheerfully toss the irreparable, don't write what you'll never salvage.

This also applies to *scene* versus *summary*. Once you compose a *scene*, if it doesn't add, will you squelch rationalization and willingly condense it to *summary*? If not, probably best to avoid developing it in the first place.

● **Does voice involve tradeoffs?**

Doesn't most everything? Just as the most exquisite rose spoils a cornfield, irrelevance, no matter how intriguing, has no place in a novel. Writing is a succession of choices. Tangential or suspenseful? Narrator or character? Now or later? Lyricism or momentum? Broad or narrow? Decide based not on your own appetite but what you suspect your audience would savor.

● **What if you have to explain something?**

Limit yourself to your best guess about what readers want, which often differs from how much you're tempted to share. Then hurry up. Avoid the abstract or didactic. Keep readers connected to the characters. Counteract info-dumps with tension, lyricism, or both.

TIP

Voice helps transform reality into story.

● **Are CP and voice connected?**

CP helps diagnose *telling*, monotony, imbalance, and false tone. Often you can address any issue you uncover by changing the CP level. Frequently, because you've altered the perspective and opened yourself to new possibilities, the process liberates voice.

⌐**Exercise**: Getting to know your narrator

Which truths can your narrator disclose? Which secrets can your narrator withhold? Imagine your narrator addressing your ideal reader. To please that person, must your narrator change anything? Does this ideal reader want anything you haven't provided? Brainstorm until you uncover the least obvious but still logical. To surprise readers, you must first surprise yourself.

⌐**Exercise**: Analyzing musicality

Model passages in your novel after stylistic techniques in fiction you love. Don't expect to find every strategy applicable. Instead, develop an ear for the techniques comfortable for your voice and genre. Keep experimenting. Don't squelch. To flourish, voice deserves a non-judgmental environment.

⌐**Exercise:** Finishing up

Admit your story's greatest weakness. Fix it.

Risking It All

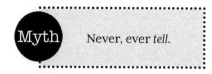

Myth Never, ever *tell.*

The ban against *telling* starts in elementary school. Call the truck "shiny" or "red"—never "terrific." Of course it's absolutely true that condescension offends, and that oversimplification, abstraction, or judgment drain prose. The best novels replace authors with narrators and answers with questions.

Deep inside story, the author surrenders control to the narrator and characters. You'll find your voice down there—unless you play it too safe. In terms of development, more than one letter separates "bilking" from "milking." Though overwrought prose irritates, writers sometimes don't go far enough, push hard enough, incorporate the most intriguing possibilities. Rules and caution erect and protect structure. But voice requires a fair amount of impulse and inhibition.

Unconsciously, and maybe consciously as well, every author must balance constraint with spontaneity. Ernest Hemingway ended *For Whom the Bell Tolls* with only scenery conveying Robert Jordan's valor in the face of death. Nothing *tells* in this finale; there's no hint of that.

But is this climax slightly anemic? Perhaps. Does it feel resolved? Again, perhaps. Every writer faces choices like this. Taste alone elevates ornament above minimalism, Beatles over Bach.

A novel's ending can be a dangerous place for risk-taking. Surely that's the worst place in a novel to *tell*. Yet if you examine the ending of a novel such as Ian McEwan's *Saturday*, you'll see that popular, award-winning authors sometimes take enormous risks in those final lines.

And that those risks pay off. If a novel captures the kind of naked trauma that McEwan's does, perhaps readers want, even need, some visible comfort. Even if that comfort involves a smidgen of *telling.*

Do abstract references automatically make an ending more or less moving than Hemingway's? The individual reader—and writer—must decide. Yet regardless of how much restraint one prefers, most of us agree that voice neither flouts nor worships tradition. And it's less about detachment than emotional truth.

Emotional truth is rarely a safe choice. This is treacherous territory, demanding from the novelist the courage that Hemingway lauded in characters like Robert Jordan. Want courage like that? Prepare to take chances. Arm yourself emotionally and intellectually, however, because you'll need both the rules along with the rationale for occasionally ignoring them.

No spoilers will happen here. But Michael Cunningham is especially deft with endings. You might want to examine either *The Hours* or *Flesh and Blood* for masterful technique at tying everything up without being either blatant or irresolute. Collect endings you admire. Analyze why you admire them. That'll assist with your own ending.

In every genre, readers not only need but welcome some abstraction, information, and illumination. Those build texture. Just don't rationalize how much you can get away with. Because either exiting from the plot or clarifying any part of it almost always entails trying to get away with something.

Balance is the key. Without a dazzling plot or reputation, perhaps you want to limit the amount of risk. That can promote the realistic attitude every novelist needs. On the other hand, by all means imagine producing The Great American Novel. But your narrator's voice comes from your own. If flying terrifies you, will you really create a narrator who sounds like an astronaut? Bravado isn't courage. Honest self-assessment is.

TIP

Charismatic voice balances risk against reality.

⌖**Exercise**: Training Your Voice

Identify three differences between paragraphs from your novel that you respectively love or dislike. Use these discoveries to revise everything in your book.

The Artifice of Artlessness

Myth

Artless writing comes from inborn talent plus a lot of luck.

In basketball or architecture, neurosurgery or law, those who excel make it look easy. No one sees them sweat. Because they perspire in private. Voice works the same. Great novels usually require years of revision to sound like casual singing in the shower— to capture the sensation of sound rather than the sound itself. Instead of inflicting commotion or boredom, art imitates those. Fiction's goal isn't realism; it's verisimilitude.

Of course it's challenging to suggest instead of replicate, or to articulate the inarticulate. Maybe it's harder still after extensively revising plot, characterization, description, style, and on and on. Ultimately, though, unless instinct overrides technique, you'll never write in the voice only you possess.

Revision culminates in locking up your toolkit to enter a Zen-like state. Listen to the voices of your characters and narrator. Let them repay the love and energy you conferred. Listen for the sound you want your novel to make. At the end, revise not from head but heart.

And so...

TIP

Never let readers guess how hard you worked to suggest you never worked at all.

Readers hear voice because, behind-the-scenes, an author struggled with everything that makes a novel more substantial and beautiful than the sum of its parts. The voices of your narrator and characters insulate you from self-consciousness and sentimentality, from preaching, pontificating, or substituting cuteness for charm.

The marriage of plot to theme and syntax to diction produces voice, but only if the narrator and characters subvert ego. That's what you give your readers, whether you find an agent or publisher swiftly or never, whether dozens or millions enjoy your novel.

You write because your novel drives you, inspires you, fills you, fulfills you. Story sustains you when revision feels hard. It's supposed to. You keep finding troubling passages and have trouble fixing them. Then, one unbelievably sunny day, the only trouble left is what your characters face.

Marketing, though, makes even revision look easy. The intersection between love and business signals trouble—yours, not your characters'. After all that passionate revision, who wants to feel like an investment? It's just business, though. Why blame agents and publishers for wanting the most money for the least risk? Give your book a chance: Don't give up too soon. But if you must, happily, self-publishing becomes increasingly easier, cheaper, and less stigmatized all the time.

Revise until your novel's done, then shop it or self-publish it. Don't wait. Don't wait to conceive its sibling, either. The best antidote for fretting over your novel's fate is starting another.

Deep Revision Tip
#10
Take risks. That keeps novels—and novelists—forever young.

Redefining "Dirty" Words

Many words are so abstract, vague, cute, tired, melodramatic, or inappropriate for fiction that unless they're used ironically or originally, they often distract from the story thread. Some of the words below have lost their power; others sound antiquated or are simply used too often. Here's a partial list to start you out.

Adorable	Painful
Agonizing	Pitiful
Anguish	Pretty
Awe	Rosy-cheeked
Awesome	Sad
Beautiful	Said
Dreary	Shrug
Extremely	Snow-white
Glorious	So
Heart	Somber
Heartfelt	Soulful
Heretofore	Strode
Home	Stormy
Jet-black	Suddenly
Joyous	Thus
Magnificent	Turn
Meanwhile	Ugly
Moreover	Very
Pain	Yearning

And now, why not add your own?

Twenty Role-Model Novels—and Why

Obviously, numerous other candidates could have made this list! The titles below merely represent some stellar choices among the many wonderful books out there.

1. Subtext: Jane Austen, *Pride and Prejudice*.

    Still the most one can say in minimal words with minimal intrusion.

2. Universal treatment of the particular: Shauna Singh Baldwin, *What the Body Remembers*.

    A psychological translation of trauma.

3. Fictionalized history of science: Tracy Chevalier, *Remarkable Creatures*.

    Dual female protagonists in a man's world.

4. Tragedy as art. Kiran Desai, *The Inheritance of Loss*.

    Exploration of power and powerlessness.

5. Imagery and motif: Anthony Doerr, *All the Light We Cannot See*.

    Poetic treatment of finding the hope within the horror.

6. Metaphor as theme: Kim Edwards, *The Memory-Keeper's Daughter*.

    Multi-layered symbolism.

7. Electricity: Jonathan Franzen, *Purity*.

    Edgy treatment of voice, plot, character.

8. Sub-plotting: Chad Harbach, *The Art of Fielding*.

    Integration of protagonist dilemma with minor character dilemmas.

9. Voice: Alice Hoffman, *The Museum of Extraordinary Things*.

    Contemporary fairytale at its best.

10. Interlocking stories: Martha Hall Kelly, *Lilac Girls.*

    Fictitious handling of actual events.

11. Point of View: Barbara Kingsolver, *The Poisonwood Bible.*

    Unique sound for each point of view character.

12. "The personal is political": Jean Hanff Korelitz, *The White Rose.*

    A protagonist ironically revealing an entire social milieu.

13. The Anti-hero: Ian McEwan, *Solar.*

    Momentum through dark wit.

14. Character Revelation: Claire Messud, *The Emperor's Children.*

    Backstory and unreliable narration for psychological analysis.

15. Theme: Tim O'Brien, *In the Lake of the Woods.*

    Emotion rendering tragedy immediate and real.

16. Poetry in Prose: Richard Powers, *The Echo-Maker.*

    The relationship between the natural landscape and the human brain.

17. Intellectual analysis: Richard Powers, *The Gold Bug Variations.*

    Delivery of scientific information in fiction.

18 Irony: Fay Weldon, *Habits of the House.*

    Historical fiction at its most informative and entertaining.

19. Art as Politics: Andrew Winer, *The Marriage Artist.*

    Haunting analysis of how the past controls the present.

20. Over-arching metaphor: Colson Whitehead, *The Underground Railroad.*

    Abstraction made concrete.

Writing Books You Probably Shouldn't Miss— and Why

So many books on writing fiction—so little time. Although many superb books aren't on this list, here's a place to start. These books profoundly affected the discussion of fiction, from arc to verisimilitude, in *Beyond the First Draft*.

Aristotle: *The Poetics*.

> Still the greatest insight into the art/life relationship.

Jack Bickham: *Scene and Structure*.

> Components of scene and how to use them.

Lisa Cron: *Story Genius*.

> Psychology as a tool for crafting fiction.

Lisa Cron: *Wired for Story: The Writer's Guide to Using Brain Science to Hook Readers from the Very First Sentence*.

> Counteracts prevalent misconceptions about how writing works.

John Dufresne: *The Lie that Tells a Truth: A Guide to Writing Fiction*.

> Motivation and structure for the novelist.

Bonnie Friedman: *Writing Past Dark*.

> Support for coping with the writing life.

David Jauss: *On Writing Fiction: Rethinking Conventional Wisdom about the Craft*.

> Essays on fiction, and particularly illuminating on point of view and the narrator.

David Jauss, ed.: *Words Overflown by Stars*.

> Analysis of prose, poetry and most everything related to writing.

Noah Lukeman: *The First Five Pages*.

    Getting your novel off the ground and keeping it moving.

Donald Maass: *Writing the Breakout Novel* (and its accompanying workbook).

    Tips and tricks to escape the predictable.

Donald Maass: *Writing 21st Century Fiction: High Impact Techniques for Exceptional Storytelling*.

    Exploding the constricting parameters of genre versus literary fiction.

Robert McKee: *Dialogue: The Art of Verbal Action for Page, Stage, and Screen*.

    Why people write weak dialogue and how to remedy that.

Robert McKee: *Story*.

    Universally applicable analysis of plot and character.

Jessica Page Morrell: *Between the Lines: Master the Subtle Elements of Fiction Writing*.

    Analysis of suspense, tension and the factors that affect them.

Jessica Page Morrell: *Thanks, But This Isn't For Us*.

    Agent analysis of why novels sell—or don't.

Sol Stein: *Stein on Stein*.

    A genre-oriented overview of fiction that's useful for all novelists.

John Truby: *Anatomy of Story*.

    Universally applicable techniques for meshing plot with theme.

CP Clarification

Character Presence (CP): Tags, Descriptions, Metaphors

● **CP5 (Context): Narrator on world. No differentiated characters. Filtered.**

- "The Professor."

- Eagle's eye perspective.

- Scenery, setting, overview.

- Distant philosophical or abstract appraisal of the protagonist's surroundings and situation.

- Observation or description without differentiated characters.

- World or physical world.

An authoritative narrator eliminates individual characters, who'll get time later. The narrator sets the scene and builds the world.

Further clarification

○ Excludes distinct individuals. CP5 (Context) can be populated, but only distantly. A crowd fleeing a volcano is CP5 (Context), but one toddler fleeing the danger is CP1 (Zoom-in).

○ Includes both neutral and filtered language. "Her car functioned as an attic," and "Fetid remnants of last month's snacks cluttered her entire car" are both CP5 (Context).

○ Covers all environment, whether setting or generalization. "The gray waves roiled," and "Oceans mesmerize" are both CP5 (Context). Their commonality is truth about the world or human nature rather than about one character.

● **CP4 (Insight): Access to character emotion and backstory through narrator. Filtered.**

- "The Analyzer"

- Observations about the characters that they may not themselves know.

- Rationale for character thoughts, emotions, actions.

- Deep analysis of character motive through narrator filter.

Narrator exposes psychological character profile to the reader. No literal physical details here.

Further clarification

○ Reveals inner character through narrator. In first person point of view, the narrator and character somewhat overlap. Still, the narrator interpretation of CP4 (Insight) contrasts with the uninhibited character response of CP2 (Mindread).

○ Excludes a literal external component. "Ida's relationships always ended in tears" captures a mental state (CP4 - Insight) rather than the literal physical act of crying. Add tangibility, and the sentence becomes CP3 (Shared): "Ida wept, fearing she'd never see him again."

● **CP3 (Shared): Character and narrator reveal inner and outer character. Filtered.**

● "The Melder"

● Everything but dialogue.

● Actions and thoughts combined.

● Interaction and its significance through both character and narrator.

● Synthesis of emotion and behavior.

● Actions demonstrating thoughts and emotions.

The narrator's still around, but the characters are very much on stage.

Further clarification

○ Includes a literal external component. Peter imagining Paul in California is CP4 (Insight), but Peter cursing N.Y. traffic and dreaming of Paul in California is CP3 (Shared).

○ Tracks perception. Sensation involves both external and internal. So a character hearing a singer is CP3 (Shared), but a character singing is CP1 (Zoom-in).

○ Involves connotation. Words like "surprisingly" or "egregious" introduce the narrator, which changes unfiltered CP1 (Zoom-in) to filtered CP3 (Shared).

○ Captures condensed or ongoing time. Fretting daily or bringing dirty laundry weekly adds the narrator, so it's CP3 (Shared), not CP1 (Zoom-in).

- **CP2 (Mindread): Intimate access to character emotion without narrator. Unfiltered.**

  - "The Toddler"

  - Blurting, spewing.

  - A punch of passion.

  - Character's gut-level emotion.

    The character bursts into erratic emotional responses, which might mean speaking only in nouns.

Further clarification

○ Includes only character thoughts. What distinguishes character from narrator? The tone and surrounding sentences.

- **CP1 (Zoom-in): Physical character behavior or description without narrator. Unfiltered.**

  - "The Actor"

  - Plot dynamics without emotional description or analysis.

  - Interaction between character and environment as it occurs.

  - What's happening.

    Only the outside of the character is visible, with the narrator completely offstage.

Further clarification

○ Includes either behavior or description. This level is anything filmable about a character, either "Sue wore a gold necklace" or "Jim clasped the gold necklace around Sue's neck."

○ Excludes *collapsed time*. *Summary* like "always" or "at every sunset" introduces the narrator, changing CP1 (Zoom-in) to CP3 (Shared).

○ Eliminates filtering. Connotative and abstract words like "disrupted" or "imprudent" involve the narrator and are CP3 (Shared), not CP1 (Zoom-in).

○ Omits perception. A character seeing, hearing, touching, tasting, or smelling is simultaneously external and internal and thus CP3 (Shared), not CP1 (Zoom-in).

Glossary

Abstract: A condition or idea, such as "fury" or "war," available only through intellect rather than sensation.

Antagonist: Not mere obstacle or opponent but impetus for summoning the best in the protagonist.

Arc: Protagonist progress from weakness to satisfaction and maturity.

Backstory: Events or emotions preceding the forward journey of the plot.

Causality: a plot where each event instigates the next, forcing characters to face the consequences that foster maturation and earn the ending.

Character Presence (CP): A system classifying each sentence excluding dialogue as a) filtered through narrator or direct through character b) physical or intangible, and c) distant or close.

Coherence: Unity of the details and events in the novel.

Collapsed Time: Condensing hours, years, or even centuries into a few words or phrases.

Concept: The heightened dramatization of the central conflict, whether quest, love affair, success story, or moral correction.

Concrete: An image one can see, hear, taste, touch, smell or any combination of these.

Connector: A *summary*, transition, conjunction, or conjunctive adverb linking a moment, detail, location, or motive with what follows.

Connotation: Language with emotional, cultural, historical, and often symbolic associations.

Deep Revision: Diagnosing and strengthening characterization and plot rather than superficial issues.

Denotation: Literal, objective wording.

Deus ex Machina: A non-believable resolution of a problem via an otherworldly contrivance that miraculously sets things right—now often called "the cavalry save."

Dilemma: A compulsory choice between two unacceptable options.

Double-Duty Detail: Image simultaneously accomplishing more than one task.

Doubling: Duplicating information, verbs, dialogue, or general and specific versions.

Dramatic Irony: A conflict in expectations arising from readers having information unavailable to one or more of the characters, e.g. long before Oedipus Rex, the audience knows that he murdered his father and married his mother.

Emotional Shorthand: Intangible, oversimplified abbreviation of feelings like "joy" or "rage."

Epiphany: In drama or fiction, the moment of insight a character achieves due to the resolution of arc. Ideally, the audience experiences this epiphany along with the protagonist.

External: Everything that happens outside the character's mind: the setting where a novel occurs, along with character appearance and behavior.

Faux Clairvoyance: Inference based on physical or psychological evidence that permits expanding point of view without overtly violating it.

Fictional World: The territory within a story or novel, which might be anything from a realistic portrayal of the past or present to a realm of zombies, fairies, or humans with supernatural powers.

First Person Retrospective: Narrator interpreting events the character previously experienced.

Foreshadowing: A hint or series of clues suggesting or foretelling what will occur later.

Genre: The category identifying your intended audience, i.e. fantasy, romantic suspense, historical literary, mystery, etc.

Internal: Inner or inside, as in a character's psychological conflict versus pressure from the outside world.

Literal: Factual portrayal of reality.

Live Time: The sensation of cinematic immediacy—moment by moment.

Logistical Overkill: Painstaking delineation of the obvious or insignificant.

Logline: A short, snappy summary of a novel's protagonist, dilemma, setting, and genre.

Metaphor: A symbolic comparison, often including a physical component; divisible into sub-categories, such as the indirect metaphor, or simile.

Multi-Faceted Emotion: A dynamic, complex, and thus realistic expression of a feeling, such as lust tinged with guilt, fear, pity, or a mixture of those.

Narrator: Persona guiding readers through the fictional journey.

Pace: The flow of information tempered by its expression.

Plot: Causal incidents escalating to external climax and internal change.

Protagonist: Central character, originally a hero, in drama, fiction, or film.

Pressure Point: Explicit external pressure necessitating action.

Showing: Events and details that permit vicarious experience and thus reader inference.

Scene: a dramatic interaction that engages reader emotions, usually involves more than one character, and changes at least one character psychologically, morally, or both.

Scene Goal: Intense, explicit character desire that impels choice and action.

Self-Talk: the first-person narrator reproducing character thoughts that could be self-evident from behavior and dialogue.

Single-Pronged emotion: An oversimplified reduction of a many-layered response like envy into superficial, abstract, unrealistic *emotional shorthand*.

Spine: Novel's backbone from inciting incident to climax.

Stage Business: Gesture, movement, or body language that expresses character feelings, often to ground, clarify, or pace dialogue.

Subtext: The unarticulated meaning that readers infer from what is implied rather than expressed through the dialogue or description.

Summary: A transition bridging or condensing the span between or within *real-time scenes*.

Suspension of Disbelief: Willingness to accept the events and characters in a fictional world as credible, however fantastical or surrealistic these might be.

Symbolic: A figurative or metaphorical comparison different from actual reality.

Synesthesia: In fiction, describing one sensation in terms of another, i.e. the flavor of Beethoven, the taste of his music.

Syntax: Sentence structure.

Telling: Dispensing judgments or conclusions that readers would prefer to infer.

Tension: The balance between opposing forces that keeps readers wondering about the final outcome.

Theme: The meaning of the characters' journeys.

Thesaurus Syndrome: Altering individual words instead of revising deeply.

Third Person Limited: Restricted to a single "he," "she," or "it" vantage point.

Third Person Omniscient: Broadened to go everywhere and perceive everything.

Tone: The verbal expression of an author's attitude toward a subject, e.g., humorous, ironic, biased, condescending.

Turning Point: A significant change in the character's progression toward the climax: nothing will ever be the same again.

Understatement: Use of a restrained tone, particularly when dealing with a tragic situation or theme.

Unreliable Narrator: The device of relating events from the perspective of a character who is deceitful, delusional, or unaware of the situation's implications.

Verisimilitude: An altered version rather than reproduction of reality, used to make fiction more credible, causal, vivid, and moral.

Voice: The combination of tone, style, and phrasing that projects an author's singular personality onto the page. This captures the illusion that in a pure and natural yet compelling way, the author personally connects with the reader.

Voiceover: The narrator addressing the audience directly, often at lower volume.

YA: Young adult fiction or nonfiction.

CP Snapshots
CP (Character Presence) Levels

CP5 (Context)—physical world through narrator. Filtered. External or philosophical.

Presence: Setting, theory, or fact from the narrator. No distinct character.
Distance from character: Furthest. Impossible to distinguish individual characters.
Tangibility: Everything from physical setting to abstract concept.
Goal: To anchor—landscape, philosophy, information.
> **Example**: Dogs save lives.

Snapshot of CP4 (Insight)—character psychology through narrator. Filtered. Internal.

Presence: Indirect narrator analysis of inner character.
Distance from character: Still far. Internal character available only through narrator.
Tangibility: Abstract except for symbolism.
Goal: To probe—revelation of character reaction, background, and choices.
> **Example**: She/I loved dogs more than anyone or anything.

Snapshot of CP3 (Shared)—character and narrator. Filtered and direct. External and internal.

Presence: Narrator and character for all-inclusive view of character.
Distance from character: Intermediate. Narrator still present.
Tangibility: Multi-dimensional.
Goal: To fuse—synthesis of external and internal character.
> **Example**: She/I petted Rover until he seemed to smile.

Snapshot of CP2 (Mindread)—uninhibited character emotion. Unfiltered. Internal.

Presence: Direct inner character without narrator.
Distance from character: Close. No narrator separating reader from internal character.
Tangibility: None.
Goal: To eavesdrop—unimpeded access to the character's most private self.
> **Example**: Dogs. Nothing like them.

Snapshot of CP1 (Zoom-in)—character behavior and appearance. Unfiltered. External.

Presence: External character without narrator.
Distance from character: Close. No narrator isolating reader from conduct or appearance.
Tangibility: Total.
Goal: To film—movie sequence of character interaction.
> **Example**: Rover licked my/her entire face.

Acknowledgements

I begin with my partner, who is surely more wise and supportive than any writer deserves. My agent, Kim McCollum of the Purcell Agency, worked tirelessly to find the right home for this book. I spent many happy years learning from and with my former colleague, Christine DeSmet—a constant source of energy, dependability, and inspiration. Angela Rydell was instrumental in critiquing early drafts of this book. Matt Corey, Amy McGovern, and Michael McGovern offered amazing insight on revising this book, particularly the CP section.

In all my years of teaching writing, I always learned as much as I taught and encountered far too many brilliant and creative minds to mention here. But I'd like to at least acknowledge those individuals who generated the terminology that's become part of my coaching vocabulary: Jan Schubert for *double-duty detail,* Kim McCollum for *self-talk,* Bruce Noble for *faux clairvoyance,* and John Strikwerda for *feeling a feeling.*

This book would never have been possible without the synergy of all the remarkable minds that have touched my own, and I can't articulate the depth of my gratitude.

Index

> "Brilliant guide provides bounty of revision tactics and solutions."
> **CHRISTINE DESMET**
> Author, Master Class teacher/faculty associate in writing and director of the
> "Write-by-the-Lake Writer's Workshop & Retreat" at University of Wisconsin-Madison

Beyond the First Draft supplies the tools to understand and polish every aspect of the novel. How do you escalate work from good to great, from a manuscript to a published novel? This comprehensive, accessible book offers not only tips and techniques, but encouragement and motivation.

How often do writers say, "What's wrong, and how do I fix it?" As a writing instructor, novelist, and writing coach, Laurel Yourke can offer expertise to every writer starved for knowledge of craft. You'll find those strategies right here.

Decades of first-hand experience inspired *Beyond the First Draft*. **What makes fiction work? Revision!** And superficial revision only wastes time. The real transformation begins when the writer examines and reworks the deep structure of scenario, scene, and sentence. Analysis, illustrations, checklists, charts, and exercises help the writer to diagnose the issues directly pertinent to a particular manuscript. Of the many writing guides on the market today, none use this combination of myths and tips to promote clarity and practicality. And since revision can feel overwhelming, the book urges writers not only to assess weaknesses, but to capitalize on individual strengths.

> "I wish that *Beyond the First Draft* had been available when I wrote my first novel."
> **JERRY APPS**
> Author of seven novels, the most recent *Cold as Thunder* (University of Wisconsin Press, 2018)

> "The growth among my student writers in understanding the personal narrative has encouraged me to acquire this book for my school and to recommend this title to other AP teachers and University of Minnesota faculty I know."
> **MARA COREY**
> AP English and University of Minnesota faculty

LAUREL YOURKE, PH.D.

Through the University of Wisconsin-Madison outreach programs, Yourke has taught classes and workshops to students from 8 to 18 to 80. Her experience includes TV, radio, and lectures in various venues across Wisconsin and other states. She has presented at major conferences over a hundred times and lectured everywhere from libraries to living rooms, not only on writing but also on fiction and poetry. Decades of coaching and critiquing every kind of writing resulted in two teaching awards: one from the university, one from the state.

Yourke is the originator of UW-Madison's renowned annual Write by the Lake Retreat, a popular writing conference currently expanded to fourteen sections with several masters' classes. This year it celebrates its 20th anniversary. Yourke continues to privately offer six different writing programs and remains connected as a consultant to the UW writing program. Yourke blogs weekly writing advice at noveltips.blogspot.com.

ISBN 978-1-942545-98-9

9 781942 545989

51795

WRITING
$17.95

Wyatt-MacKenzie Publishing
DEADWOOD, OREGON